Contents

Life on the Tundra:

A Strange and Quirky Existence

by

Janet Marie Jacobs

DORRANCE
PUBLISHING CO
EST. 1920
PITTSBURGH, PENNSYLVANIA 15238

Dorrance Publishing Co
585 Alpha Drive
Pittsburgh, PA 15238
Visit our website at *www.dorrancebookstore.com*

Interior Design by Tracy Reedy

ISBN: 978-1-6442-6222-1
eISBN: 978-1-6442-6404-1

Thank you to the many people
who helped make my book a possibility.

First and foremost, to the love of my life
and partner of 25 years, Jill,
who supported, encouraged, proofed, and
took care of the details while I wrote.

To Renée and Janet Mitchell,
for their input on content and proofing,
and Tracy, who laughed and cried
his way through each chapter.

Chapter One

Skating the Tundra

Skating was as much a winter's past time as swimming was in summer. Every Christmas, someone got a new pair of ice-skates. When we were very small, little double blade metal ones were fastened over our boots. When I was six, I got my very first pair of brand new white lace ups with the single blades; the kind the big kids wore.

At that age, no winter seemed colder than any other. We were, after all, flatlanders. We were used to six months of frigid winters in the North Country. Those winter outings required enough clothing for six kids. It was usual to wear long underwear, two pairs of socks, a pair of pants, two shirts and a sweater, all underneath a snowsuit. Then came the two pairs of mittens, the hat, and the hood pulled up and scarf tied so that it covered half of your face. Needless to say, it took outside support to dress you, and lord, help the child that didn't remember to pee before the process was started.

For Christmas of 1962, we left Rome, NY. There we were, seven of us in my dad's Volvo. It took about three hours to arrive at the "Outlet," a small remote town on the St. Lawrence River in Canada.

We made the trip to join our cousins for Christmas. The families were close and my aunt and uncle had been asking for years for all of us to spend

1

the holidays with them. Finally, my father (the one hold-out) decided if we were going to go, it might as well be now!

When we arrived, we were greeted by my aunt and uncle and their seven kids. I watched as my uncle grabbed my father by the hand, patted his shoulder, "Jake, you were waitin' then until you had five and we finished with seven!" Dad laughed and so did my mother and aunt.

We kids were chomping at the bit to say hello; we hadn't seen them since last summer, and between all of us kids, we ran into the rambling Queen Anne style house and were quickly informed of the sleeping arrangements. My sisters were still babies and so would be sleeping with Mom and Dad. My brothers, Joe and Jack, would sleep on the floor of the boy's room with their cousins, Andrew and Jeremy. The oldest, David, would sleep in his room, next to the bathroom, and the littlest cousin, Ian, would sleep in the bathtub, not that there was any need for him to do that, he just liked sleeping there. It was his special place to sleep when company stayed at the house. I was just one addition to my cousins, Elizabeth, Claire, and Erin, so I got a space in a twin bed with Claire.

Over the next couple of days, we took sleigh rides, built snow forts, and raided each other's snowball stashes. It was an idyllic Christmas vacation. Most memorable was my debut in my brand-new skates. While my cousin tied up the laces on my beautiful new white skates, the boys shoveled an area of the frozen river in front of our cousin's house and created a skating rink. Everything was wonderful. I watched my older cousins do figure eights. We made a chain, flinging the last kid off into a snow bank. I spotted my father in the window holding one of my sisters while he watched us skate. I waved to him. He smiled and held my sister up to the window to see us. Pretty soon it was my turn to be last; the one that my cousins would throw off the chain into the snowbank.

The sky was brilliant and the sun shot glare off the snow, so it was almost too bright to look at. We were laughing, red cheeked kids, and I was having the time of my life. In the next moment, I felt myself descending into the icy cold river, quite unable to comprehend what was happening in those first few seconds. Panic entered the core of my body as I became engulfed in the frigid and soundless river, the only light being the circle of daylight I had left behind a moment before. As I looked up at that circle of sun light above me, I could see the water form a soft crystalline structure which meant I would be sealed in a tomb of ice. Time stood still. My brain was assessing where I was and how I got there. Any movement I made with my arms seemed in vain with all the heavy clothes and my new skates. Thoughts ran through my head at a constant, yet slow pace. What seemed like hours was but seconds. Even as time began its forward motion again, it started only slowly, as though I were in that river for a very long time. As an adult, I realize it was mere seconds before my cousin David's hand exploded into that opening and grabbed the shoulder of my snowsuit. It wasn't until I was yanked to safety that my eyes and skin stung from the cold. Time regained its regular pace, and frightened out of my wits, I cried and spit river water.

David ran with me in his arms to the house, squeezing me so tightly I felt like a rag doll. I saw my father running, slipping, to meet David. His arms out stretched, he grabbed the front of my snowsuit, like I was a suitcase, and lifted me out of my cousin's embrace. He pulled off the wet scarf around my neck and worked at unlacing my skates while he ran to the house. I was crying and I heard him say over and over, "Talk to me Jan," but all I could do was cry, that sniffling, snot nose, unable to speak kind of cry. I heard my father say in a soft and low voice, almost a whisper, "You're ok now, stop crying or your snot will freeze on your face." I could hear my uncle's angry voice to my cousins about a fishing hole, a hole not old enough to freeze over completely and not marked.

It's strange how certain memories will stay with you forever and the age you are when things happen determines their ethereal or dreadful qualities. The only thing I feared then and fear now are being trapped beneath ice. Swimming underwater has always made me look to the surface, to be enchanted, with some reservation, by being beneath it. Even in my 60s, I dream about that plunge through the ice, sometimes catching myself on the edge of the hole and other times sliding just enough off center for David's hand to reach in vain.

When I was 19, I left the north east for San Diego, CA. I left at the end of one of the worst blizzards, ten-foot high snow drifts and our usual winter fare with bone chilling winter winds. I was determined I would never go back to live in the frozen tundra ever again. I gave my sister my favorite winter jacket.

When I arrived in San Diego, I stayed with a friend. The night I arrived, we sat in her Jacuzzi and I looked up to see a clear sky with brilliant stars and palm trees. I left behind a temporary government job I'd been at for two years in New York State; it ended only days before my trip. Within a week of moving to San Diego, I had a job at the Arctic Submarine Lab. It was also a government job at a very small military installation on Point Loma. I worked with Admiral Lyon, famous for his exploratory missions to the Arctic and the Antarctic. Sue, my supervisor, showed me a huge pool, completely frozen on the surface. They needed someone to record statistical information from the dolphins, swimming to retrieve potential explosive devices in the Arctic waters. The first day on the job, I thought of the tank as my worst nightmare, but each day got a little easier because I was concentrating on what I was recording rather than manipulating a childhood memory. It was a wonderful job, and I loved working there, and before I knew it, four years had flown by. The job ended and I was out hunting for work again.

Going through old cards and letters one day, I stumbled upon a letter my dad wrote. It was a response to a letter I wrote to my father after my first day of work at the Arctic Sub Lab. I talked about the irony of working in a place that would be front and center of my childhood trauma. His response was the shortest letter I ever received from him. "Dearest Janet, I am in awe of your competency and resilience, which will be with you as long as you nurture them to stay. Love, Dad."

Chapter Two

Music of The Heart

Sometimes someone impacts your life in a way that alters how you look at the world, simply because of who they are, how they've lived their life, and the love and trust they've shown you. I am lucky enough to say that I have a couple of people in my life like that. One is my partner and another is my father. They are part and parcel of who I am today.

My father was born Charles Edward Jacobs on June 23rd, 1918 in Girard, Ohio. He was the oldest of four children, though he only knew one brother Bill and one sister Janet, as his siblings. The youngest sister, Ruth, was given to his mother's sister to raise. Chuck, as his family called him, had a very difficult childhood. His mother Annise and step-father Walt were alcoholics and very abusive. My father, in remembering his childhood, would tell us the many times that he and his siblings went to bed without so much as a piece of bread all day. His parents moved from Girard to Carbondale, Pennsylvania and finally to Pittsburgh, Pennsylvania where his mother's family resided.

For seven years, he and his brother were raised by his mother's oldest sister, Margaret. She was the youngest teacher and only woman to act as principal in the history of the Pennsylvania Public Schools. He adored his Aunt Margaret and she instilled in him lessons of love and family. We were not allowed to say her name without reverence and a nod to her vocation as the youngest and only female principal in the history of Pennsylvania Public Schools!

His complicated lot in life was made even more grueling and sad with the death of his little sister, Janet, from pneumonia two days before her fifth birthday. He told us kids about this time of his life with, "I thought I would never feel happy again. Her death left a hole in my heart that took all of you to fill."

By 17, he'd left home and worked as a coal miner, a golf caddy, and finally joined the military in what would become the Air Force. His brother followed him into the military. During the war, my father traveled to the South Pacific, Africa, Asia, and Europe. His brother Bill was stationed in England as an American addition to the Royal Air Force and on D day brother Bill was killed when the glider he and fellow soldiers were in was shot down by the Germans. The death of his brother could make him stop mid-sentence to regain his composure. They were as close as two brothers could be and the loss of his brother was incomprehensible to him. My father was part of a group of soldiers to liberate the Nazi death camps at the end of the war. He had a photo album of this liberation that was kept in a cupboard, high up beyond our reach. However, when I was about nine, I snuck a look at it and was terrified by what I saw, unable to sleep for weeks.

In 1993, I contacted the Jewish Historical Society. They were looking for survivors of the death camps to tell their stories on video. I told them my father was one of the liberators and he had pictures of that. They wanted to know if he would be willing to give his account of that time. I called my father and he would not, but he was willing to donate the album to them. They accepted that and his pictures were placed in the archives of the Holocaust Museum in Washington, DC.

My father married at the very end of the war and had two boys. Charles Edward and a son named after his brother, William Thomas. As adults, he told us a little bit about his first wife, that she had cheated on him and he divorced her. His sons never kept in contact because his former wife "Margaret" had spoken very badly of him. One son, Charles, came to our house only once, looking for money from our father. I was about five, and I remember it because the tension in our household was incredible between my parents and my father and his son. We never saw either one of them again.

When my baby sister was living in San Diego in the early 80's, she found out from one of our cousins in Albany, NY that the youngest son, William, went to her church. My cousin inquired about his last name and discovered that not only did he have the same last name as my father, this was my father's son! She asked where his brother was living and was given his address in San Diego, right across the street from my sister! I really wanted to meet these half-brothers of mine. I urged my sister to contact him, but she wouldn't. So, I did. I called one evening and asked to speak with Charles Jacobs.

He identified himself as Charles and then I said, "Do you have a brother William, and father, Charles Edward?" His response shocked me.

He replied, spitting the words into the phone, "I don't have a father." I gave up at that point, his answer spoke volumes about his lack of desire in wanting to know anything about his father or us. The effort would have just been lost on him.

Growing up with my father was interesting and fun. He was a good man with the soul of a child. He was probably the extreme opposite of my mother. My mother was wound pretty tightly, and my dad had a very relaxed view of the world. When I asked them how they met, my father said that the G.I. bus depot in Rome, NY was an outdoor place. It was next door to Western Union, and when the weather started to turn cold in the rain and ultimately the snow, the gals at the Western Union Office next door invited Jake, as he was known then, and his fellow G.I.s inside to stay warm and dry. My father was immediately smitten with this attractive gal, who was easy to talk and laugh and absolutely the fastest on the typewriter that he had ever seen. They started to date, and did so for almost two years, and were married on June 1st, 1948 in my mother's parent's garden. My oldest brother was born a year later.

My father's first military assignment after marrying my mother was to London, England, where my middle brother was born. My father had to be there ahead of his family, so my mother took the baby on what used to be a troop ship and sailed off to England to meet my father. In recounting that time, my mother said it was a ship filled with new wives and babies to meet their spouses but that the voyage was punishing, crossing the rough waters of the Atlantic on such a small ship!

The two lived through a few historical and domestic events. My mother watched Queen Elizabeth's coronation in 1953, a year after brother Joe was born. The worst case of smog in the city of London took place in the 50's and effected hundreds. The domestic events included my oldest brother getting very sick. My mother stayed home with the baby and my father jumped in the car with Jack and went roaring off to the hospital. On the way, Jack got sick all over himself and my father took off his clothes, threw them in a field, wrapped Jack in a blanket, and continued his trip to the hospital. Whenever my parents spoke of the event, my mother would ruminate about a perfectly good set of baby clothes that my father did not bring home, even 40 years later!

My father was king of bargain hunting as a young guy, only to hone his skills to a high sheen by the time the grandkids arrived. While in England, he discovered a farmer with a miniature horse and he haggled with the farmer for the horse and a cart for Jack's birthday. My mother, however, did not want any horse in their house, no matter how good the deal was, and alas, my father was forced to return said equestrian and wagon to the farmer.

My mother's recollection of England was that they had a house that over-looked the White Cliffs of Dover. The house was used as a morgue during the war with autopsies performed on the long wooden drain board in the kitchen. The weather was windy and cold all the time and the bar across the street was noisy in the evenings. My father's recollection was that the scenery was beautiful, the people were warm and charming, and the pub across the street was always filled with laughter and song. My father said that whenever he tried to get our mother to join him at the pub, she always responded with, "Jake, I have two babies to take care of."

After England, my father asked an acquaintance in the Transfer Office to see if he could get three years in Alaska. In 1955, he and family were on their way to Fairbanks, Alaska. While going there was a dream come true for my pop, it would also be one of the hardest years for both of my parents, having lost a child and his beloved Aunt Margaret in 1955. In 1956, I came into the picture and my father especially recounted my arrival with great fanfare and joy, whether he did so as the father announcing to all the family in New York that they had a new little bundle of joy or for the 20th time to friends.

While my father loved England, he positively adored Alaska. He was a great outdoorsman, hunted, fished, camped, hiked, and generally got to know the countryside and wild life. He worked as a medic for the military with a search and rescue/recover unit. If a G.I. was lost or checked out a plane and didn't show up as his flight plan had indicated he should, then my father would gather his team and go looking for them. One G.I. took a small plane out on the open tundra. When he did not return, they went searching for him. They found him, the plane, and a polar bear all dead in a horrific bloody scene. The G.I. landed, having trouble with the plane, and while he was working on it, a polar bear spotted him and charged. All the man had was his service revolver with six shots, which he emptied into the bear, but the bear killed him before it walked away and died. Not long after my father arrived in Fairbanks, three guys from the base were driving an old truck used to haul supplies when a bull moose stepped onto the highway from the brush and the truck hit it head-on. The moose was dead but so were the G.I.s without much left to the front of their vehicle. My father's stories of Alaska were prolific and my parents made some good and lasting friendships there.

My dad was a man of great physical strength. He was a boxer, welter weight, for some of his time in the military. But nearly every day of his life, he did something physical and encouraged his kids to be physically active. When my brothers and I were very young, he would take us to the gym to watch him work out. In particular, I remember him using the rings and holding an "iron cross" position, which required enormous power.

My dad was all in favor of his kids taking risks or trying new things. He could usually be found at my sporting events, field hockey, basketball, or base-ball. At ten, I went to a survival camp. It was a week long and I learned how to survive being on my own in the wilderness. When I saved up to buy my first bike, he went with me, sending me off on my own for eight miles to home. I was 11. He would spot my baby sister in the backyard while she practiced gym-nastics. Joe started lifting weights in high school and challenged my father to a "lift the front of the VW bug contest." He gladly obliged his son, my dad walking away the winner. When my middle brother wanted to sky dive, he was there watching, probably holding his breath, but he was there.

At 18, I started running with my brother and father. Even after months of training and loving the feeling of speed that my body could perform, our father could out run both of us; my father was 56. When I wanted to take flight lessons, he encouraged me to go ahead with them, even when I told him I wanted to use them to be a bush pilot in Alaska.

On an emotional side, when my sisters had productions at school or with their scout troops, he was there, too. He carefully saved my sister Joan and brother Joe's art work they had given him for Christmas. When my oldest brother and younger sister had babies, he gladly cradled them in his arms. His much-loved Aunt Margaret had taught him about love and family, and he had learned those lessons well.

The things that I and most people remember about my father are his sense of humor and his music. He was usually the life of most every party and people loved to hear him sing. For having such a tragic childhood, something that could define him as an adult, he chose to find the absurdity and wit in life.

My father loved music. He had a beautiful voice and his voice was a constant. I heard my father's voice in song as much, if not more, than speaking, in our household. His voice sounded most like Perry Como, a fellow crooner from Pennsylvania. He sang when he was happy, calm, trying to cheer you up, celebrating the holidays (he had songs for every holiday) or just to sing. He courted the love of his life over and over with his songs. I don't think that a day went by that I didn't hear his lovely voice. I couldn't imagine a time in my life when I wouldn't hear his amazing vocals again.

In the 1950's and 60's, there was a television show called the "Jimmy Dean Show" and my father sang on that. When I asked my mother if she saw him on the TV, she responded, "No." I asked, "Why not?"

She answered, "Janet, I had three kids to take care of."

My father was a romantic and would grab my mother away from her ironing to dance with him to a special song. Sometimes he would pick me up and place my feet on his shoes and dance me around the room. We would listen to his music and learn all the words, and he would in turn, learn the words to our music. My father knew who The Beatles and Creedence Clearwater Revival or Judy Collins were, just as we would know who Bing Crosby, Mel Torme, or Rosemary Clooney were.

It's been ten years since my father passed, and while the intensity of the grief has changed, I miss him more than I can say, but I am amazed at the legacy he left behind, for even though he is not here in person, I can, at any time, summon his voice in my head. I can see him dancing with my mother in our dining room or singing White Christmas as we put up the Christmas tree or grabbing my mother for a spin as she was getting ready for church on Easter Sunday while he sang "In Your Easter Bonnet." I feel lucky that way. Sometimes he thought I wasn't paying attention, but I took in every note and every stanza from him. And from this man who had a very difficult start in life, he derived the greatest pleasure in leaving his family with riches far beyond any of our understanding.

Chapter Three

———

Flatlanders

*A*fter having lived in San Francisco for 37 years, I was smitten with the beautiful Golden Gate, its hills, with their wonderful sweeping views, the interesting history of the Bay Area, and the weather with its micro climates everywhere. If you didn't like the weather in one part of town, all you had to do was go to another part of the city. Usually,one could find cool and fog or sunny and warm! I felt so spoiled with our weather; it was mid-range of what I looked for to live in, hovering between 40 and 80 degrees. Occasionally, we'd get a day that would be as high as 100 degrees, but that was rare. Winters also might send some ice our way, but again, that was rare. Suffice it to say that it was not at all like my hometown and that was perfectly alright with me.

My home town, Rome, is a town of about 25,000. It's the geographic center of New York State and one of the main stops on the Erie Canal route. It gets all four seasons, with winter being the longest at about six months. The weather, during those six months, is unequivocally of the subzero variety. Winters there are severe and not meant for human life forms. The land is flat everywhere you look, and because we are flatlanders, we get wind that just gallops in from Canada and the great lakes, causing temperatures to plummet to bone chilling levels. If you've ever lived through one of these winters you know, without a doubt in your soul, that hell has a lot more to do with lake effect winds and subzero temperatures than it does with fire and brimstone.

Rome's history included fur trappers and Fort Stanwix, a log cabin fortress built to protect the fur trappers and families from the Indians and the British. Another piece of history is that Francis Scott Key, author of the Star-Spangled Banner, was buried in Rome.

History that you might not hear about would be the biggest outbreak of Giardia or Beaver Fever in the U.S. Their contaminated reservoir sent scores to the hospital and had the populace boiling water for the better part of a year!

As far as industry was concerned, Rome was pretty significant. Rome Wire and Cable was famous for *Romex Wire*, found on nearly every construction site across the U.S. Revere Copper and Brass had a lighted sign on the top of the factory with Paul Revere galloping on a horse in colored lights. We saw it every time we drove to my grandparents. Oneida Ware was also made and sold there, and Griffiss AFB was a substantially sized air base with lots of troops and lots of ethnicities.

In the 1980's and 90's, the stores in downtown and uptown began closing their doors at a record rate. Some of the industrial business were farmed out to China. Utica and Rome were among the fastest shrinking cities in the U.S. according to the national news. The city Fathers decided that answer lay in tourism. I'm not sure how they arrived at this, but they were optimistic that if they reconstructed Fort Stanwix in the middle of downtown and built a pay parking garage to accommodate all these tourists, it would definitely be the answer. When the tourists didn't show and Romans became angry having to pay for parking where it used to be free, the city reverted back to free parking. The city fathers were wringing their hands because the tourist attraction blunder backed up and did a full-on ramming speed effect to the city budget. Rome became a city with more parking than it had stores or people to shop there and all free; a concept as remote as Nepal in a city like San Francisco.

After the tourist disaster, people began to look for jobs elsewhere. No wonder, long winters and a haggard economy. People wanted to leave the area, and leave they did like lemmings over a cliff!

Winter time during my 2nd grade was brutal. On Monday mornings, the heat in the school was turned back on, but it took till Tuesday to actually get warm. All the little girls froze to death. We were allowed to wear long pants under our dresses, but the principal eventually insisted that we were to remove the slacks under the dresses when we arrived at school. I refused, and my teacher called my parents to tell them I was out of line. My father picked me up and was actually the one who came up with the idea of wearing three pairs of thick tights under my dress. I went back to school warm and happy.

At Christmas time, everyone, including us, the one Jewish household on the block, decorated for Christmas. We pulled out our decorations and watched our dad put up the Christmas lights. He would come in the house after several hours, stomping the snow from his boots and cupping his hands over his mouth and swear that next time the outside decorations went up, my brothers would be doing it! After my oldest brother moved out, the job eventually fell to Joe and me. I was not at all familiar with Murphy's Holiday Law, which specifically states that the only day you have to put the lights up shall be the coldest day of the year with a wind chill that will make you feel like you are strapped to the nose of a 747 at 30,000 feet!

To all of us kids, winter, of course, was all about tobogganing, skiing, skating, snowball fights, but somehow our parents always managed to include shoveling the driveway in the mix as well.

The best spot to go tobogganing was William's Hill on William's Road at William's Farm. All the local kids were there with their sleds and saucers on the weekends. My brothers, sisters, and I would slog through knee deep snow, hauling our toboggan to the top. We all piled on and it ripped down that hill like an E ticket ride at Disneyland! One good bump and we were airborne, legs, arms, hats, and sometimes teeth flying. On one trip down, my sister bit right through her tongue, ending a very short day of sledding and changing her speech for a little while.

Christmas time when I was ten was special. My father bought a ping pong table for the whole family, which he set up in the biggest room of the house, the dining room. So either you were at the table eating, playing ping pong, or sitting under the ping pong table watching TV! It made for cramped quarters, but it was fun for the five of us. In this Christmas of 1966, we also got hit with the biggest storm ever. The school system generally allowed five days off from school each winter–weather related days. This year we took all five snow days at once, right at the tail end of two weeks off for Christmas and New Year's. Three glorious weeks is what we had off. My parents were beside themselves. Their tempers sored sometimes because if there is one thing that doesn't mix well, it would be five very active kids and two adults with extremely limited coping skills.

We were anxious to get outside and play. The space between our house and garage was about four feet with no roof. It had a ten-foot drift in it. We had to shovel our way out the back door. The snow was so high, we could take our saucers to the roof of the garage and sail into the back yard where we'd sink into five-foot high snow. There was much fun to be had, but eventually my parents insisted we find the cars and shovel the driveway, which we did for all five days straight while it continued to snow.

While we had some great fun in winter, it was also punctuated by times when we were housebound; when the weather was just too horrendous for anyone to venture out. My cousins, who lived on an old farm, said that the barn was far enough away from the house that they had to string a rope from the house to the barn in order not to wander off and freeze to death.

When we had white-outs and the weather was that bad, my parents didn't let us go out, so I would hang out in my closet and look at the maps to try and figure out where I wanted to go when I left home. I was an outdoor kid and winter weather made me feel antsy. I constantly read about places that were warmer. Hawaii looked pretty good, warm all year round. Australia was a possibility, even if their seasons were reversed. New Mexico also seemed to be a contender.

When my father retired from the Air Force, the military would pick up the cost for him and his family to move anywhere in the U.S. he wanted to retire. One morning, I came to breakfast with my atlas and was pouring over facts about New Mexico.

My dad looked at the book and casually commented, "I thought about retiring there."

I looked up, "You thought about it?" I was shocked.

"Yes, I thought it would be nice there."

"But instead you chose Rome?" I sat for the longest time in puzzlement. I couldn't quite believe what I was hearing. "But wouldn't the military have paid for you to retire there with your family?"

"Well, yes, of course."

"So why did you choose Rome, Dad?"

"Oh well," he was very matter of fact, "Your mother wanted to be close to her family." I looked at Joe, he raised his eyebrows with a question mark behind them. My oldest brother raised his hands like a scale and said live in New Mexico, and raised that hand, or live in Rome, New York and lowered that hand.

16

My father gave a little smile and went back to his paper and coffee. It took me forever to get over the fact that my father actually made a conscious decision to live in Rome, N.Y. That was the first question mark I remember placing in my head about my father's judgement. After breakfast, I went back to my closet and started a new list of places I would move to when I left Rome, reviewing the maps, the economies, and average temperatures first.

When spring vacation rolled around, Romans exited en masse to any place that was warm, usually Florida. Six months of snow, heavy winter gear for yourself and your car, shoveling the driveway (pre and post snowplow), enduring 20 below wind chill factors, and skating their vehicles all over the road would make anyone go a little crazy. When the masses returned, the kids showed at school with a golden-brown tan. Since my family was not one of the sane crowd, tripping to Florida or the like, I could usually be seen in gym class with my blinding white skin. Envious is what I was. Dammit, just one year I wanted to see palm trees and come back to school with golden skin.

One year I discovered a product that was supposed to tint your skin and make it look like you had a golden tan. Well so, I wouldn't see palm trees, but I would have a tan. I spread the stuff on my legs and positioned myself on the couch with my legs propped on the arm. I had to keep my lotioned parts from rubbing on anything because it would make the tan uneven. I explained the situation to my brother who decided he wanted a piece of the couch, even though there were chairs and the floor, but he wouldn't relent. After a shoving match, he accidently spilled his Coke on one of my legs. I jumped up to wipe it off, but the damage was done. The Coke interacted with the tanning lotion, and well, one leg was perfect and the other perfectly streaked, it looked like I had peed down my leg. It took about a week to fade. In gym class, it was painfully obvious that my family had not trekked to Florida during vacation. I was grounded for two weeks for skipping gym class and had one occasion of detention, for the same.

Chapter Four

Life on the Farm

All year long, we made regular trips to Uncle Harold's and Aunt Irma's in Earlville, New York, a small farming community. My father rarely came with us, except on holidays. The road to and from Rome and Earlville was well traveled. About half way in the trip, we passed Attica prison. I don't know why, but I was fascinated with it. When I was very young, I asked my dad if they let people visit.

My father said, "Only at certain times and with a lot of people watching their visits."

"Why do people watch their visits?"

"Jan, its full of people who wouldn't think twice about hurting you. That's why they're there, so they can be locked up and not hurt people."

My brother chimed in, "Hey, Dad, maybe we can sell some girl scout cookies there!"

My father smiled a little, looked in the rearview mirror, and said, "Be nice to your sister, Joe." There were times when I hated my brother so much, I just wanted to pummel his tiny little head. My mother had enough and she hollered "Jake!"

"Come on you two."

"Dad, she is flicking my ear!"

"You're such a baby!"

"Daaaddd."

"Both of you stop it!"

At night, the place was illuminated. Anyway, the prison meant we were either half way to Uncle Harold's or half way home.

Uncle Harold was my mother's oldest brother. He tended to be a smart ass and really very obnoxious. My dad didn't like him at all. He only went on the holidays because he knew there would be other family members there whose company he enjoyed. Aunt Irma was a saint and we loved her. She shielded everyone she could from Uncle Harold's constant criticizing and mouthing off.

They lived in a 100-year-old house with a small barn in the yard, which leaned profusely to the left and looked, for my entire childhood, like it was ready to fall to pieces. It finally did when I was in my 20's. Their house was situated on a corner in the middle of Aunt Irma's two brothers, both of whom were dairy farmers. Other than the three properties, there wasn't a building in sight that resembled any kind of civilization. One of Aunt Irma's brothers up the road had one son, Craig. The other brother down the road had six boys. Jerry was my age, Michael was next to him, and Mark was the youngest. Mark was blind, but he navigated around the property so well, he could amaze you. Out of six boys, these three were the ones we hung out with the most. The three oldest boys worked the farm with their father.

Whenever you arrived at the house, you entered by way of the old mud room, which was filled with old barrels, canned goods or canning supplies (depending on the season), coats, boots, hats, laundry, and a variety of small ancient implements I never could identify. Also in the mud room was the smell of old potato and onion skins, food cooking, whatever my cousin had just killed in hunting season, fresh milk, and Aunt Irma's warm embrace. I say warm because she was a big woman who worked like a dog, and she generated a lot of heat. She was my favorite aunt and I loved her dearly. I also loved that house with all its smells.

My cousin Diane was Aunt Irma and Uncle Harold's youngest. She was eight years older than I, yet she was the closest thing I had to a big sister. She was smart and loving and I adored her. She was also a big woman, like her mother, and when she took you in her arms, there was absolutely no question that she was hugging you. She would fix my hair, include me in her group of friends, and give me the attention that I couldn't find at home.

While the visit was known as a "trip to Aunt Irma and Uncle Harold's," it was really Aunt Irma and Diane that we were there to visit with. Uncle Harold had a propensity to give everyone a nickname, whether they wanted it or not. It was like he couldn't bring himself to call them by their given name. My mother was Jimmy, sister Julia was Twiggy, sister Joan was Mia, my brothers were Elvis and Buddy, cousin Diane was chicken (really?), Uncle Lawrence was Oscar, Uncle Harold's grandkids were Mica and Claire, and on and on it went. Interestingly, my father and I did not have a nickname and I was happy with that. Uncle Harold and Uncle Lawrence (aka Oscar) were the two brothers of my mom, who fought continuously and the same two my father had kicked out of the house on numerous occasions.

Sometimes my other aunts, uncles, and cousins came to visit for the holidays, and when the meal was done, the men would adjourn to watch TV with uncle Harold, and the women would stay at the table to talk and joke uproariously about everything under the sun, not sparing anything or anyone. I loved my gender during this time because the little boys were generally shoed out of the kitchen to be with the men, but all the girls could remain with the women. I listened with fascination as my cousins and my aunts compared childbirth experiences. I was allowed to ask questions like, "How did you meet uncle so and so?" Memories of courtships were brought up, which lead to the difficulties of marriage. Aunt Irma would say love is blind and someone else at the table would respond with, "It's deaf and dumb, too," and the women would roar with laughter.

So much information was passed around at the after-dinner talks that it was difficult to keep up. "Remember Mr. and Mrs. Stewart from Toronto, he worked with Pa (my grandfather), well, he passed away six months ago and Mrs. Stewart..." Those women relied on each other as outlets to diffuse the stresses of marriage, good or bad, kids, the work, the boredom, and any other thing that they were lugging on their shoulders.

In the winter, the weather made it prohibitive to play outside. There wasn't much to do but hang out in the house and watch Diane play Frankie Valle records with her friends. But in the warmer weather, we could go visit either farm, get a squirt of fresh cow's milk, hang out in the barn, and get into all manner of mischief. There were two horses that roamed the pastures. Diane would coax the horses to the fence, so we could ride them bare back. One afternoon, when I was very young, Diane petted the horse while my brother hoisted me on its back. The warmth and power of this massive animal was scary to me. Diane suggested I lean forward and hold on to its mane while it trotted around the pasture. My cousin, however, decided that the situation called for more excitement and slapped that mare squarely on the ass. It took off and me with it. I held that mane for all I was worth and closed my eyes while it transported me to the far end of the pasture in mere seconds. I always felt fortunate this was not my only experience riding a horse, but thanks to my cousin, it was the most exciting.

During an afternoon of sheer boredom, we began a game of hide and seek. A couple of us took off for the silo, which was accessible from the second story of the barn. The silo had double Dutch doors. Both parts of the Dutch door were closed which meant that the silo was recently filled with grain. Not realizing this, I opened the bottom door and my cousin opened the top and several hundred pounds of grain flowed over us, knocking us down and sending us about 20 feet back. We got up, stunned, and surveyed all this grain on the top floor of the barn. We all knew instantly that this was a very bad thing to have happened. The boys' father, however angry he was, calmly told us that he would have to spend a lot money to have the grain pumped into the silo again and did we know that we could have been killed? He sent us back to Aunt Irma's. We all waited for the other shoe to drop. I was sure my life was going to end at a young age, but Aunt Irma never said a word about it. This soft spoken, very stern sounding man was raising six boys, he ran a huge dairy farm with the help of his sons, brother, and nephew, and here come these ignorant city kids causing trouble and ultimately costing him time and money. What puzzled us was he never said a word to get us in trouble. Once I even asked Diane, as an adult, if he ever mentioned us playing hide and seek in his barn and having to pump grain into the silo again. She looked at me with surprise and said no, hoping I would tell her the story, but I didn't.

The only child of Aunt Irma's brother up the road was Craig. One summer day, about a week before we were to return to school, Craig and I were out in his father's barn. He wanted to show me the new milking machine that his father just purchased, not that I was all that excited about milking machines, but I figured Craig was since he talked about taking over his dad's farm. One moment he was talking about this machine, and the next he was asking me if I wanted to go to the state fair with them on Labor Day weekend.

"What?"

"My family is going to the state fair. Do you want to go with us?"

"Yeah, I guess so."

We walked out of the barn and up to the house and sat down in the grass on the shady side. It was a sweltering summer day and I kept pushing my hair off my sweaty face. Without any warning, Craig kissed me on the mouth. I looked up at him in surprise and he kissed me again, sticking his tongue in my mouth. I knocked his shoulders back away from me.

"What are you doing?" I screamed at him.

"I thought you would like it."

"Well, I don't. It's gross."

The truth was it wasn't so bad; he just caught me by surprise. I hadn't ever kissed a boy before, and my friendship with Craig represented only a tomboy-ish interest until then. The look on Craig's face was one of devastation and I instantly regretted yelling at him. I looked at him and he looked away, we sat in silence and then he did it again, this time without any objection from me. As easily as that, the entire dimension of our camaraderie had changed.

The trip back to Rome that night was suddenly different. While I had always viewed boys as partners in baseball or football, I never thought about one this way before. I talked to my mother about the state fair and she had given the ok. I didn't tell her about the kissing. I couldn't wait to see him again. It felt rather exciting.

A couple of days before the Labor Day weekend, my mother received a call from Aunt Irma. While a call from Aunt Irma wasn't so unusual, my mother calling me aside after was. Craig was taking his dad's tractor back home after helping his uncle when the tractor went a little too far to the edge of the road and into the ditch; it rolled over on Craig, crushing his skull. My mother spoke the words to me. The words echoed in my head, but it was as if my brain could not comprehend them, they were just sounds. I want a do over is what we said in baseball, and in my head, I kept saying to myself, "I want a do over." I rolled over in bed and grabbed my pillow when I heard my father come in the back door from work.

He whispered my name, "Jan."

"Yeah?"

"Want to have some cheese and crackers with me?"

"Ok."

We went to the kitchen and I got things out of the fridge and cupboard as if by rote. I sat up with my dad many times. We sat eating and not talking. I lined up the Ritz crackers and Dad put small cheese squares on the crackers.

"You kids go back to school next week?"

"Yeah."

"Did you get some new outfits for the year?"

"Yeah, a couple."

"How about we take a drive to Lake Delta tomorrow?"

"Ok."

"We'll bring some stuff to cook on the grill?"

"Ok."

He stopped chewing and looked at me. "Don't feel like talking much?"

"No."

My eyes began to fill with tears. "Jan," I looked up at his face, "I heard that you lost a very good friend."

"Yeah."

"I'm sorry about Craig. I think I understand what you must be feeling." I just stared at the crackers and cheese. "When I was a kid, not too much older than you, my sister Janet passed away." I looked up at him. "She was four-years-old, and two days away from her fifth birthday. I didn't ever think I would feel happy again. I loved my sister a lot, like you love your sisters, your cousins, and your friends. As you grow older, the people in your life that you love either pass from old age or illnesses or accidents. It's not fair that they can't be with you forever here on earth, but that's the way things go. What you should remember is that they may not be here on earth, but they are with you in spirit, and when you pass, you will see them again."

"Really?"

"Yes. In the meantime, they watch out for you."

"They do?"

"Yeah, but your job is to be as good a person as you can be, so they don't have to spend all their time watching over you."

"I'll never see Craig again."

"Oh, you'll see him again not until you pass, which may be a long time from now, but you'll see him." I did feel somewhat better. Not a lot but a little. We talked about going to Lake Delta, I got up and kissed him goodnight. I laid in bed, awake for a long time, trying to imagine what a crushed skull looked like.

The service began with Craig's casket closed for obvious reasons. While morticians can do amazing things to make the dead look good, there was just no rebuilding the head and features of a 12-year-old boy who was pinned beneath several thousand pounds of tractor weight. I was numb for most of the day and then felt the most incredible sadness for years afterward. For a long time, no one talked about Craig dying, except Aunt Irma and Diane. True to their warm and loving natures, they would remember him out loud and cry at his absence, it was a great source of comfort to me.

After a while, I resisted going on trips to Uncle Harold's, but when I did, I didn't seek out any of the other kids, just hung out with Aunt Irma in the kitchen or sat in the yard, wondering if today was the day that barn would finish falling over. Craig's death had unnerved me in a way that I couldn't explain for a long time.

Chapter Five

Relative Sanity

Spring held so much assurance, mainly that we'd be out of school in a matter of weeks. Everyone was planning his or her strategy for the summer vacation. My mother had applications for vacation bible school, but when the one and only day came to register, my brothers and I managed to be absent until well after the registration time; and since you had to sign up in person, we managed to skirt vacation bible school for another summer.

By the time school neared its last week, Romans were usually smack in the middle of the tropics. It was already 80 at 8:00 in the morning and the Japanese Beetles were singing, which meant it would be another scorcher. I sat in class on the sunny side of the building, not moving, breathing as slowly as possible, the sweat pouring off me. The tundra had turned into some twisted equatorial nightmare with not a palm tree in sight, just the vast humid flatlands of Rome. It would have been tolerable if we could have spent the day at Lake Delta, but parents and teachers frowned on this, so here we sat in this miserable heat. I kicked off my loafers and started fanning myself. There was absolutely no reason to be here except to get a head count, so here we sat for 45 minutes.

I vowed, at the end of seventh grade, that wherever I went, when I left Rome, the temperature would be warmer than the winters and definitely cooler than the summertime hell. The cut off would be 85; nothing above 85, nothing lower than maybe 35. I could live with 35, there wouldn't be any snow or maybe a light dusting, and if you had to make a quick run outside for something, you wouldn't have to dawn every piece of clothing you owned against the cold. California came to mind. I read about San Diego, the average temperature there was 72 degrees; I could live with that. Palm trees would be nice, too. I had a picture of San Diego and there were lots of palm trees. Palm trees would become an important symbol of nirvana for me. They represented a great departure from the frozen ice cap of Rome in the winter, never mind that they could grow in the most arid and tropical environs.

Rome was a bust in the summer except for Lake Delta, where one could picnic and swim and the St. John's Fair, which was the major summertime celebration. It offered the usual rides: the Ferris wheel, the tilt-a-whirl, and the swing. If you twisted the chains of your swing and hung on to the chair next to you, pushing off when the ride was at full throttle, it was as close to flying as a kid could get.

After St. John's Fair, the only good thing about Rome was getting out of it. My mother's family was from Canada and my grandparents had a camp on the St. Lawrence River across from Canada. The camp was about 30 feet up a hill from the water front. It was in a small quiet cove that sheltered us from boat traffic. The only structures in the area were a silver airstream belonging to my grandparents, my parents' tent, a small tent that Uncle Lawrence put up, and a large tent Uncle Harold erected for his family every year. The official name of the land was called Dead Man's Cove, but when Uncle Lawrence, my mother's younger brother, and Uncle Harold, her older brother, bought the land, then it became Watson's Cove. My mother was so pleased they used the family's name that she painted a wooden sign with "Watson's Cove" and put a big red arrow pointing, by mistake, in the opposite direction to the camp. It proved to be confusing to friends and other family visiting.

It was a perfect place for a kid or adult to relax. We could swim, fish, boat, and the weather was cool enough for a sweater in the morning and evening, and the cold river made the heat bearable during the day. The area was called the Thousand Islands, but the number of islands actually totaled 1,400. I was determined I would see each one, keeping a record book of the islands we visited until one of my cousins dripped all over it after a swim and the pages of islands sort of ran together, forming a very long obscure peninsula.

In 1962, my parents sold their two-bedroom, 50-foot trailer to Uncle Lawrence. My parents bought the trailer originally to weather the last two stations in my father's military career, Maryland and New York. When my parents bought the trailer, there were only three kids. When they sold it to Uncle Lawrence, there were four kids and one on the way, so they bought a four-bedroom house on Lee Street in Rome.

Uncle Lawrence, the classic over achiever, hauled this 50-foot trailer up through the woods and dirt roads (barely there) and plopped it down where his tent used to be. Forgetting child labor laws, he corralled my brothers, cousins and I into helping him build a porch, fireplace, and dock. Uncle Harold stood by watching all this happen, occasionally emptying his pipe on the construction site, and decided that a permanent platform was good enough for his family to erect their tent on. It took him years to build that. Uncle Harold thought his brother was an idiot to spend money and effort on his summertime home.

The banter between the two would last all my life. Uncle Lawrence was a self-made capitalist. As a teenager, he sent for a kit to make a TV, opened a TV shop where he sold and repaired TV sets. Uncle Harold was a mason. He and my grandfather worked together for many years on such buildings as my high school, two elementary schools, the post office, art center, and library in Rome. Both Uncle Lawrence and Uncle Harold knew all there was to know about their trades. They were both skilled, but they couldn't give accolades to each other. Everything was a competition between the two; they never gave the other an inch of slack. Even when it seemed they might be getting along, you would hear, "Kiss my ass."

At the river in the morning, I'd wake to the smell of coffee, freshly made doughnuts, and warm scones that would melt in your mouth. My gram was an excellent baker. The things she turned out were incredible. The milk was in a glass bottle with the cream on the top that she scooped out and spread onto scones. I'm convinced that my battle with cholesterol today probably started on these mornings, but I wouldn't trade those taste memories for anything. Everyone was sipping their tea and coffee and eating breakfast while the low drone of a news station from Ottawa sounded on the radio. Mornings like this were priceless. My cousins didn't arrive at camp until a couple of days after me, so my grandmother doted on me, and since I was sent to camp without my parents, there was no screaming to be heard, sometimes for as much as a month at a time.

As soon as I could, I'd make the run from the trailer down the hill to the water. Since I was the only kid for a few days, I'd spend the first several days trying to better my own time. I'd run down the concrete steps, past the flowers, the bucket rusted out beneath the water pipe, over a huge slab of pink marble, around a tree, and down the last set of stairs, one calculated jump from the rock, and onto the dock I stepped. Thirty-two seconds was the time. I envisioned a new Olympic sport "hill racing." Several ten -year-olds lined up and the gates are opened, they dodge all manner of obstacles, steps, boulders, tree stumps, and the first one to the dock wins. This time it was me! I held my arms in the air while the crowd cheered, the cove otherwise silent.

To say that we spent a lot of time in the water would be a gross understatement. After the grueling hour, post meal waiting period. If we weren't in the water morning, afternoon, and evening, then we were on it. We swam the length of the cove and beyond, climbing the rocks and sunning ourselves for a while before making the swim back. After a swim, we'd lay on the warm wood of the dock, where I would imagine sunning myself on the beaches in California with Annette Funicello and the Beach Boys. I would have a golden-brown tan all year round.

If we weren't swimming, we were fishing from the dock. The fishing rules were clear, you kept the hooks out of human flesh, you baited your own hook, and ten or older, you cleaned your own fish. My uncle was determined that fishing would teach us patience. What it taught me was the art of "catch and release." I had absolutely no desire to practice cleaning one of the little buggers. My cousin, who was seven, was the only one still stock piling my grandmother's freezer.

One of the more bizarre rituals around this sport was the early morning fishing trip. My uncles were up and on the river by 5:00 a.m. Breakfast happened after the fishing was over. Their bickering continued whether they were in the same boat or separate ones. The calm river was picturesque with the sun coming up. Water bugs were skimming the surface of the water, and it was so quiet, you could hear the fish jump and the loons sing, and then you'd hear, "You're full of shit, Lawrence" or "Awe, go to hell, Harold." I usually sat at the opposite end of the boat, wondering why they always picked me to accompany them on their early morning fishing trips while my cousins slept in their warm beds. My mother's instructions to me before going off to camp was to keep my uncles company on the early morning fishing trips. Maybe she thought they might not fight as much if I accompanied them. She was sorely mistaken on that account.

On one occasion, I was sitting peacefully with my line in the water, trying to block out the two grown men verbally sniping at each other from their respective boats. When I felt a breeze and splattering of water over my shoulder and looked up in time to see a perch hit my Uncle Lawrence, dead center of his chest, with Uncle Harold in the other boat, laughing hysterically. Next thing I knew, I was under orders to take in my line and Uncle Lawrence stood up, hell bent on heading to Uncle Harold's boat. At first, I thought he was looking for something to throw at Uncle Harold. With horror, I realized he wasn't slowing and was headed directly for him. It's amazing what goes through your head in a moment like that. Panic followed by a clear understanding of where you are in relation to the shore, and more panic when you realize that you're pretty far from it.

I was ready to yell at my crazy uncles when the boats bumped violently side-to-side, and I heard Uncle Harold say, "The kid's in the boat."

Without thinking, I blurted out, "Yeah, the kid's in the boat." Both of my uncles started laughing. Whatever eruption was at hand was temporarily diffused. We pulled away and headed in. Insults were still being thrown about, but I was so relieved we were still above the surface of the water and safe that I couldn't even tell you what was said. All the way in I kept wondering if I was really related to these two idiots, maybe I *was* adopted. After that, I began to fake being asleep and unable to rouse for those early morning fishing trips.

These two uncles of mine continued to carry on, constantly one-uping each other. Uncle Harold untied Uncle Lawrence's boat and it was found one early morning, gently bumping on a large rock in the middle of our cove. Another morning, Uncle Lawrence filled Uncle Harold's row boat with water and we discovered it four feet beneath the dock. On the fourth of July, Uncle Lawrence took a run to Canada to buy fireworks and bring them back to camp illegally. During the time he was gone, Uncle Harold pilfered all of Uncle Lawrence's underwear and threw every pair of them in a patch of poison-ivy!

Hikes were almost a daily event. While my uncles' verbal altercations were mostly laughable, we needed to have our own spot away from the grown-ups. So, we packed knapsacks full of stuff. Important stuff: compasses, string, pocket knives, rabbit's foot, joke book, binoculars, a package of M & M's or a Hershey's chocolate bar and marbles (the cat's eyes were too valuable to leave behind). Those hikes allowed us complete freedom from the adult world.

If we followed the main dirt road to the end of the peninsula, past the last camp, there was a clearing there and grass where we would sit and talk, play marbles or cat's cradle, and tell jokes. It was an easy walk and I imagined that the trees were the giant Sequoias of the Northwest, where the temperature in the summer would be in the 80's and the winter might barely reach 32. Ok, so it wasn't the perfect spot, there was a lot of rain in the Northwest, but the Sequoias were awesome. My cousins kept telling me that they were just pine trees. I ignored them. Lack of imagination is a terrible thing.

The other favorite hangout was out to the tip of Watson's Cove. Our camp was dead center of the cove, and the only camp there, and nothing but woods on either side out to the point. It provided a good deal of fodder for a child's imagination. This hike was a little rougher, going over rocks and through the woods. A pile of boulders formed the clearing at the mouth of the cove. From that vantage point, we could look back to camp and see my uncles arguing or watch my grandparents sitting in the shade, chatting and playing cards. With the binoculars, you could look out over the river, spotting boats, freighters, and liners going up and down the channel. We'd stay there for hours inventing games, making up a language or hand signals to use around the adults.

While fishing was something to pass the time and keep my uncles entertained, and hiking was a break from the adult world, boating was an activity absolutely treasured by everyone, or at least it was outside those psychotic early morning fishing trips with the odd couple. We had a canoe that we rowed around the cove in and points beyond. The uncles were the owners of the pretty boats, though. Polished wood and metal that sparkled in the sun. These boats had steering wheels and two seats up front, like a car and a wooden bench in back. My uncle would take us for afternoon jaunts around the islands to see Boldt Castle, St. Lawrence Seaway, or the Thousand Island Bridge. They would point out Wellesley Island (one of my great uncles lived there with a band of Gypsies in the early 1900's). We would cruise by the shortest bridge in the world - a foot bridge about 48" long connecting two islands, one island in Canada and the other in the U.S.

People sat on their lawns, kids played on the dock or in the water, some places rustic looking, others very modern. When I was very little, I used to think that my uncle knew so many people on the river because when we went past, they would always wave at us and we would return the gesture. We passed the old yachting club from the 1920's and went around the inlets where my uncles would fish and see gorgeous clusters of lilly pads and frogs. We heard stories about the inlet areas, how during prohibition rumrunners would hide out in the Thousand Islands because these inlets were good covers from the law. We'd watch the tankers and liners go through the locks, coming from or going to the Great Lakes or Atlantic Ocean.

One afternoon in mid-July, both of my uncles packed everyone in the two boats and we took a ride out to the shipping channel because Queen Elizabeth's Liner was coming from the Atlantic Ocean through the Seaway toward Lake Ontario. It was rumored that she would stand on deck and wave to everyone. I envisioned her standing on deck in this long flowing white gown, complete with long white gloves and her crown, waving and looking somewhat like the Barbie I had received for Christmas, but we just saw a very polished ship glide regally past. My cousin leaned over to remark that she was probably having a royal piss and couldn't give a royal rat's ass about anyone wanting to see her. It was kind of a bust. I really wanted to see that silly old Queen.

As the expedition progressed, the number of boats of all sizes gathered to watch the Royal Yacht go past. I never really saw so many people and boats on the river at the same time. The break from the boats began to get bigger and bigger until there were huge waves rolling us around, or at least they looked huge sitting on the bench in the back of my uncle's boat. I was a little panicked and quite sure that these waves were going to send us to a watery grave. My uncle, while surprised at their size, scoffed that my uncle in the other boat "didn't know what the hell he was doing." Uncle Harold was standing in his boat, shouting something at Uncle Lawrence; my cousins and I just looked at each other, rolled our eyes, and hung on, each of us thinking the same thing: We just couldn't believe we were related to these buffoons!

Chapter Six

Fire and Family Disclosures

$\mathcal{I}$n the summer evenings, the residents of Watson's Cove would celebrate the closing of a summer's day with a campfire. We had a ring of rocks in a clearing half way between the trailer and the river. My uncles cut up some trees and the stumps were painted on top and served as chairs around the fire. The ritual of the campfire has become so ingrained that I do not feel as though I've closed a summer day camping without a fire. It was a time when everyone got a chance to tell a story, laugh at my uncles or they at themselves.

The ability to articulate a good story was not taken lightly and we heard many of them. A great deal of family history was given in this way as well. Whether it was accurate history was anybody's guess. Without fail, someone would leave out a pesky detail or insert a date that was most certainly a figment of their imagination and the battle would begin. Today, dates are still a fuzzy thing, but we got the basic deed down.

In 1910, or maybe 1911, a photographer showed up at my grandparents' house with a camera. My aunt had the picture and apparently was the only one with the correct memory as well. There they were side by side, my Aunt Em, Uncle Harold, and Uncle Hubert, three, two, and one-year-old. This would digress into how Hubert was always the "golden child" and my Aunt Em and Uncle

Harold got the shit end of the stick. From this my uncles would launch into what a bossy bitch Em was and the fight was on.

When my grandfather was a child, he watched from his grandmother's upstairs window as one of his uncles jumped from a wagon, pulling another man from his wagon to the ground and beat him with a railroad tie. The details on that were naturally sketchy, but somehow Uncle Harold could fill them in when everyone else couldn't, even though he hadn't even been born yet.

In 1925, the Watson clan decided to move from Brockville, Canada to Rome, NY. I sat, mindlessly watching my marshmallow burn. Diane, sitting next to me, gently maneuvered the stick out of the flames and blew the fire out. After hearing the story about the Watson Clan, I realized that *they* were the ones who started life in the dismal wasteland of Rome. I was interested to hear why. After the part about how they loaded every trunk and stick of furniture onto a rickety raft to cross the St. Lawrence River, my aunt Em, 17-years-old, was scared to death that she and her brothers, along with their belongings, would sink to the bottom of the river.

I finally asked, "Why?"

"Why what?" she responded.

"Why did Grandpa pick Rome?"

"Well, it is the geographic center of the state and he was working as a mason all over New York State, so living in the center made it easier on him." I couldn't hold back.

"Couldn't he find work in Canada?" I asked.

"How about California; there was a big migration to California in the 20's, didn't he want to live out west? What about Washington State or Oregon, he could have become a lumberjack. He could have been a mason in Utah or Arizona, help build the Hoover Dam in Nevada or a riverboat captain on the Mississippi. Didn't he ever think about Australia? He could have been a sheep farmer and owned a ranch as big as Rhode is. He could have drilled for oil in Texas. That was a big thing to do in the 20's. How 'bout..."

My brother elbowed me, and I realized that I had gone a bit too far. My father was giving off that glare that illuminated his face and drilled a hole directly to your brain, which translated to "one more word and you'll regret it." Everyone around the fire was looking at me, mouths open in shock. I fell silent while my uncle started another story. Damn, it was my father's judgment that kept us in Rome, but it was my mother's family that started the whole thing.

This particular night, Uncle Harold told us how he had done a bit of venturing. He explained how he took his family from Rome and moved them to Arizona, where his youngest daughter, Diane, aka "Chicken," was born. When they moved back from Arizona, they settled in Earlville, NY, a place only a quarter as exciting as Rome. What my mother told us later was that his oldest daughter diplomatically referred to him as the "grouch." Every woman in the family disliked him, that is except my mother, she was his favorite. He berated everyone, especially his wife and kids. Uncle Harold was seen as a miserable thing. His oldest son, Eddie, committed suicide by hanging himself in the silo of his uncle's barn. Armed with all this information as a young child, I wanted very much to ask about Eddie. I loved Eddie, he would play with us, but we knew that the topic of Eddie was absolutely verboten. I was always amazed that not one memory of Eddie was ever verbalized around these campfires except by his sister and mother.

My cousins and I continued to listen to tales of life in the rural Canadian outback or about my great-grandfather, who was a trapper in the 1800's. We heard about families of eight girls marrying into a family of eight or so boys, who ran away with whom, and left their mates with all the children. My favorite tale though was about Uncle Joe (one of my grandmother's two brothers), who lived with gypsies on Wellesley Island. It was scandalous because they weren't married, but they had children and a lot of them. My aunt and uncles remembered visiting them there. My brother was named after him. In 2010, I took my mother to visit with her nieces and nephews in Gananoque, (pronounced Gan-an-ock-way) Canada one last time. One of those nieces hosted a family reunion and I met cousin after cousin who was the son or daughter of Uncle Joe, the gypsy on Wellesley Island.

My uncle used to say that knowing your family history gives you a sense of belonging. Aunt Irma would add "for better or worse" each time and all the women would quietly laugh. As a kid, I was curious about our family's history, but my cousins steadfastly refused to partake in questions with me, feeling that "too much information" was not necessarily a good thing. I wanted to think about my ancestors as upstanding people. Some of the stories told though did not necessarily make one think they were.

When I was in my 20's, I told my cousin that I was doing some family research at the archives in Ottawa. She asked me why and I told her I wanted to know more about these people. She very seriously told me that I might not like what I found, but I did it anyway and some facts bore themselves out in the census records. One year, a wife with two boys was there and the next census she wasn't, but the two boys were with their grandmother (this was the story of my great-grandmother running away with a logger). In one census, a husband was there and the next census he was with another woman. I don't think (aside from my great-great-uncle belting a guy with a railroad tie for unknown reasons) that too much has changed in the scheme of things. Come to think of it, even my brother fit right in with the rest of the hooligans in the family. A guy cut my brother off in heavy traffic. Not satisfied with giving each other the finger, they pulled off at the exit ramp. Both of them got out of their cars, with their starched white shirts and ties, began rolling around on the side of the road. Who's to say there wasn't a similar horse and buggy incident with my great-great-uncle to provoke him to resort to a railroad tie? Tempers are a peculiar thing in the family. My cousin used to say later in life, when referring to our clan, "You can't always tell a book by its cover," but where our family is concerned, leaving that book on the shelf is probably the wise thing to do.

Chapter Seven

——

Of Mice and Barbie

When I was young, I was obsessed with Barbie, not because I wanted to be like her, but because there was so much anger and turmoil in our household, she provided the perfect means for me to act out the tension that was going on at there. Obviously Ken, Midge, Skipper, and Scooter helped with this, too. The bottom line was that the women ruled the roost in my imaginary household as they did in the real household and as they did in every Watson women's household. These were not women that stood obediently by serving their husband's whims and orders. They created a ruckus and no little one at that. They made sure that no one felt too relaxed or too at ease with themselves or their surroundings. They lived by such Calvinistic virtues as "deprive yourself," except that they added their own addendum to it, "and be very pissed off about it." Other rules of the Watson order were to control. Be in control of everyone and everything, and even if you are out of control, don't ever admit to it; an apology was considered a weakness.

The Royal Highness of Control Queens was my aunt Em. She made most everything from scratch. She made her own clothes and her kid's clothes. She even knitted clothes for my Barbie entourage. She crocheted the doilies, knitted the blankets, made every one of the Christmas decorations, and the Christmas cards as well. In some respect, she was the consummate "Martha Stewart" before Martha Stewart came along. Regardless, we hated visits to her house because no matter how warmly you dressed, you had to unload the winter para-phernalia in the garage before you came in, so that nothing in the house was dirtied. Once defrocked in the garage, you arrived in the house colder than when you started. We were instructed to keep quiet and stay on the plastic covering the rugs and not mess up her handmade doilies on the furniture. When a table was set, by God, it was set properly, no matter how impromptu the meal was, and damn your soul if you spilled something.

Her husband, Uncle Harry, did not fit into the Watson clan at all. He was well mannered, never said a bad word about anyone, was very quiet, a southern gentleman from Virginia, and just generally a nice guy. It seemed like Aunt Em was always telling him what to do and he just did it. He was the most tol-erant man I ever knew. His daughter would stand in back of his seat while he was driving, patting his baldhead and singing. This always amazed me because it wasn't a behavior my father would have tolerated, not even for a second.

As we grew older, Uncle Harry grew quieter, and in his own quiet manner, began to have little breaks with reality. Aunt Em committed him to the mental institution, where he used to work and where my parents still worked. One af-ternoon, my mother came home from work freaked to the rafters because her workday visit with Uncle Harry had yielded discussions of "severed heads" on Uncle Harry's part. My father suggested she not visit with him anymore and she didn't. So, there was uncle Harry living in the institution where his family and former coworkers passed him in their daily work, but no one would take an interest in him, except his wife, who visited.

The day that Aunt Em was informed that Uncle Harry died, she had a stroke while on the phone getting the news. For the first time in my life, I re-alized there was way more to their relationship than just a controlling woman and a henpecked man as the family had contended. It made me very sad that no one else seemed to see that.

My aunt continued on in rare form after the stroke. She had trouble with her speech and was confined to a wheelchair but managed to lock her son in the basement when he went down for laundry because he had done some-thing to anger her. She couldn't verbalize well, but she wanted to make a clear statement about her anger. She also pitched fits when my mother came to help her out. The grand finale filled the air with hair rollers, bobby pins, and other items because my mother just wasn't getting some idea she was trying to convey. It was then that my mother decided she had had enough and never went back to help her.

"If they piss you off or make you uncomfortable in any way, leave them high and dry." It was a motto embraced by the Watsons and replayed over and over again in the family.

Chapter Eight

The Ties That Bind and Gag

Who I looked like began to take on major proportions by the time I was in third grade. One brother and sister very much resembled my mother and the other brother and sister, my father, but I didn't look much like either, and people commented to that effect loudly and often. The comments made felt cruel to me and hurt. My brothers would stick up for me, but when my father witnessed such a conversation, he immediately stepped in and remarked in a fashion to make the person feel stupid, that "I was indeed his number one daughter," and that would usually end the discussion.

One of my friends had a theory that since I was born in Alaska that my mother must have consorted with an Eskimo there. It was my eyes; I had eyes that looked like an Eskimo's eyes. While I had some serious doubts about my mother having sex with an Eskimo. I just tucked the thought of it away in the recesses of my brain.

I had a serious overbite, somewhere in the range of the Grand Canyon from sucking my thumb. While it's somewhat embarrassing to admit, I sucked my thumb for the first ten years of my life. My parents tried everything to get me to stop, from threatening me, to putting iodine on my thumb, but I persisted. Well, it was a thing of comfort in a very uncomfortable household, but that aside, at the end of fifth grade, I was fitted into a pair of braces. This wasn't your ordinary set of braces, but top and bottom with rubber bands on the side and a set of prongs on the roof of my mouth, to teach me to swallow correctly and stab my tongue if I didn't. At night, I wore the headgear. Which was designed to give my jaw maximum torque. In other words, my jaw and teeth really ached all the time. The thumb sucking though, came to a screeching halt. There wasn't a way I could fit my thumb in my mouth anymore.

The first day I got the braces, my brother and I went grocery shopping with my mother and she sent me off for some Tang juice. With a mouth full of things other than my teeth and tongue, it never occurred to me that I needed to learn how to enunciate again, but Tang was not the word to start on. I had to ask one of the grocers where the stuff was, and when he didn't understand, he asked another fellow to see if he knew what I was saying. He didn't either. The humiliation was indescribable. When I didn't show for a long time after going for something as simple as Tang, my brother was sent out to find me but too late to rescue me from the extreme embarrassment of the situation.

My brother, not one to miss an opportunity, realized he had stumbled on a gold mine of potential fun with my new braces. The dinner table didn't resound with my father laughing at my witticisms about my brother's intelligence anymore, but to clicking sounds followed by, "What's up, Doc?" or "Would I like some bubble gum?" "Metal mouth," or "Tinsel teeth," "How dangerous it would be for me to get near a magnet." It was painful to realize that my father was there just to enjoy the entertainment, not regulate it. After one too many brawls with my brother and my mother's screaming on the upswing, limits began to be set about what was ok to say and what was not.

In time, I learned little tricks that would annoy and puzzle my nit wit brother. I had rubber bands that hooked to the top and bottom braces. I would use the top set of braces as a launch to send flying rubber-bands at my brother's head. It was a hoot and the best part is when I was sitting with my sisters (not fans of my brother). I gave that rubber band a really hearty launch just to make sure it stung like hell on his saved little head.

Not long after I got the braces, I stumbled on a theory about how my looks fit into the scheme of my family and confided in my best friend. It was simple; I was a twin. I had sketchy details for a long time of a sister that had died at birth in Alaska. I thought for most of my ten years that I lost a twin. It was a way that I felt connected to the family, probably the only way. Sitting outside with my father one summer night, he told me the reality of the situation. I had a sister born 11 months before me. She did not live. Her lungs were damaged and were filled with holes. She lived only two hours. I abandoned the "twin" theory and decided that maybe my best friend was right; my mother must have had an affair with an Eskimo.

It wasn't until I was 16 and my oldest brother asked me to help him put together a 25th anniversary party for my parents. Trying to locate my dad's family in Pennsylvania was a challenge since we knew next to nothing about his relatives. Jack remembered Dad mentioning a cousin in Pennsylvania. She was the daughter of Aunt Flo and Uncle Dan who visited us a couple of times in Rome. Flo was a sister of Annise (my father's mum). My brother worked him for details and then made a call to a cousin we never met to invite this cousin and her family to join the celebration.

Her name was Ruth. She came by herself. As the weekend went on, there was a very serious discussion going on and pictures being exchanged between Ruth and my parents. She and my father thought of each other as cousins. Dad, Mom, and Ruth sat at the dining room table for a while, talking in a very hushed tone. I was in my room listening. What she was telling my parents was that she was the youngest child of Annise and Walter Jacobs. Ruth wasn't a cousin, she was our aunt and my father's youngest sister. They were dirt poor and could not afford to feed another child, so Ruth was given to Annise's sister, Flo, who had one daughter of her own. Ruth never knew that Flo was her aunt and no one said anything until Flo passed. One of the aunts gave Ruth the information, as well as her birth certificate, which listed Annise and Walter Jacobs as her parents. Ruth had been given an envelope of pictures her parents, my father and their other two siblings, William or Bill and Dorothy Janet or Janet, who died at four, and lots of letters.

My father called out for me.

"Jan, can you make a pot of coffee?"

"Ok."

"Did I hear Jack drive up?"

"Yes."

"Why don't you and Jack join us."

"Alright."

Jack was living on the outskirts of Rome where he worked. He had a motorcycle and came over almost every day. Joe and the girls, Joan and Julia, had gone to the mall. Once all of us settled at the table, I walked out to the dining table and quietly waited while my father passed Jack and I pictures that Aunt Ruth brought.

One of the pictures was of my father. He must have been not much older than one year. He was in a filthy looking diaper only. His little body was dirty as well, and someone had placed a policemen's hat on him. I knew my father and his siblings had a very tough life. They were very poor. His mother and step father were alcoholics and abusive but looking at the photo of this neglected and abused little one tore my heart out. I said nothing. I passed the picture to Jack and I could see he was just as upset as I was. The picture was somewhere in Pennsylvania, maybe Pittsburgh, and the street was torn up and filthy with coal soot. He gave it back to Aunt Ruth. In one photo, dad's brother Bill and his sister Janet stood side by side. My father looked at this picture for a very long time, after which he got up and was gone for a few minutes, returning with a few of his own pictures. He handed one to Ruth.

"Janet got pneumonia and passed two days before her fifth birthday," said my dad as Jack handed the picture of Bill and Janet to me and I passed it back to my father. The picture haunted me because she was so young. Dad then handed his picture to Ruth. Ruth took the picture from my father of Joe and me in Alaska. A big smile lit up Ruth's face, then my dad smiled and held both of them together for Jack and I to see. The picture of Bill and Janet standing together looked just like Joe and I standing together. We looked like the same two children some 40 years apart.

"You were named after her, Janet, but I don't think we realized how much you look like her! You even have the same haircut! And look, this is crazy, Joe looks very much like my brother Bill!" My father was clearly happy about this.

Ruth looked at the two pictures again and remarked, "If you didn't know differently, you would have thought the picture of Bill and Janet were the same people in your picture, Chuck."

When we met our aunt for the first time, everyone commented how much I looked like my aunt, this aunt from Pennsylvania that I never knew existed until now! I thought to myself, I don't really think I look like Aunt Ruth. What we did have in common was Laplander eyes, but now I knew absolutely who I looked like. Thinking about the time period before the braces, one can see that the over-bite altered my looks considerably and that my facial features had changed drastically after the braces.

I turned to Jack, "Well, at least I know I'm part of the gene pool!" He and my father laughed, knowing full well what I had been through the last six years or so.

When I showed my partner a picture of my father at about age 40, she mentioned how much I looked like my dad. I could see my face in his. It was comforting to hear it though.

My father died in 2008, he and my mother had been together 60 years. One evening in her apartment, I could feel my mother staring at me from the kitchen. It wasn't a casual look but a locked-on radar stare. I looked back at her and smiled. My mother seemed to come out of her trance and said, "Janet, you look just like your dad."

I remember my father used to recite an old German saying, "Nowhere are there more places to hide than within one's heart." When he said this to me, it was because he knew what it felt like to not belong, both as a child who didn't look like the rest of her siblings or as adults with differences that would remain unresolved within the family.

Chapter Nine

Oh, Canada

In the early part of the summer, my cousin Dave would take his dad's motor boat and come to Watson's Cove to visit and take my two cousins and myself back to the "Outlet" on the Canadian side of the St. Lawrence River. The "Outlet" was a rural area near Gananoque, (pronounced Gan-an-ock-way) where most of my mother's family settled. They were of solid Scottish stock – the people my mother used to say who broke their backs clearing the land to plant and farm, and my father would quietly retort with, "That's because they were too stubborn to travel a little further and look for a good piece of land." You couldn't deny they were committed to the land. A bit of the farming lust still lingered as evidenced by the gigantic swath of land each family devoted to a garden. Store bought produce was unheard of. Everyone was capable of making huge summertime meals just of those things they grew in the garden and most did.

Many of the buildings in the town were built by someone in the family. The family had masons and carpenters in abundance. There were houses whose walls were witness to many generations of the same family. They were refurbished with all the modern conveniences, but their age was stamped everywhere. Queen Anne styles with wavy glass, heavy oak doors separating the rest of the house from what used to be a pallor, old decorative glass doorknobs, and the mud rooms with rows and rows of shelves, crammed full of every kind of fruit or vegetable. By early fall, tomatoes, squash, green beans, corn, raspberries, strawberries, lingonberries, black berries, rhubarb, apples, peaches, nectarines were in jars and on display and ready to eat in the mud rooms.

The canning process was one that everyone was caught up in. If it was summer or fall and you were in the vicinity, you canned. You prepared jars or helped in some fashion. My aunts had us washing jars, peeling fruit and vegetables, laying out row after row of dishtowel, or handing them freshly washed jars for sterilizing. I could never imagine how one family could work through as many jars as were stacked on the shelves of those mudrooms. I wondered if they ever tired of the process, but year after year, it would continue and each year those jars would empty, only to be filled again.

Raspberries were a mainstay: raspberry jam, raspberry cider, raspberry sauce, and raspberry wine. Every year, one of the great aunts sent us home with raspberry sauce for the Christmas pudding. It wasn't that there was a shortage of raspberries in Rome, it seemed like a thing of your mother is so far from our family, here, take her this and she will feel connected and she will have something to eat with the Christmas pudding, mind you, we were only two hours away!

One year when I was 12, one of the great aunts in her 80's, Aunt Mae, was boiling up the raspberries. There was a massive pot on the stove, bubbling the raspberries to a fine syrupy mixture. Great Aunt Mae always greeted the "wee" ones who came to her house to help, but today, she seemed frazzled and departed the kitchen, walking anxiously through the house. After several minutes, she yelled to my cousins and I to stir the raspberries. We plunged the wooden spoon into the sweet smelling, bubbling mixture and immediately felt something jingling around in the bottom of the pot. Everyone gathered around and we lifted a small gold wristwatch out of the raspberries. It was a Timex, but the "takes a licking and keeps on ticking" apparently did not include boiling in a pot of raspberries.

As the years went by and the great aunts kept getting greater, we would find various items in the raspberries: rings, bracelets, silverware, money, and miscellaneous trinkets. But eating the raspberry sauce over the Christmas pudding came to a screeching halt for me the year we found Aunt Mae's teeth in the pot. We had no idea how they could have possibly gotten there, but there they were, bumping around in the pot. My cousin screamed and threw them into the sink. They didn't look like anything Polydent could fix and they never did fit her quite right after that.

The Outlet was a world of children. Several family members had large families and were related, which probably encompassed half the town. A trip to the Outlet meant, certainly, that there would always be someone to play with. Thinking back now, it might also have meant there was some inbreeding going on, but I loved them all just the same, even though these relatives were a strange group at times.

Uncle Robert, my grandfather's brother, used to be in the Scottish Royal Infantry in WWI. Every so often, we would see him hike out at sunset to the rocks, overlooking the river, and he would fire up his bagpipe. While it looked and sounded quite romantic, we had been in the house when he blew it to life on the front porch, nearly making us all deaf and scaring the little kids. My aunt sent him packing to a spot well away from the house.

One of the aunts, Gracie, was a saver and so was her husband, Uncle Gordie. In today's vernacular, that very well could mean hoarder. He saved tools, farm implements, and old engines. She saved most everything under the sun, thinking that there would be a use for it one day. A trip to her house, the one she lived in for almost 80 years, was like a trip back in time. "Life" magazines and newspapers from the 30's and 40's adorned her garage. Pictures of relatives from the last century were everywhere. She had whole drawers devoted to bundles of letters she had received since she was a child. She saved baby shoes and clothes from her children and her siblings. We could play with one of the very first monopoly games ever made or with a china doll Aunt Gracie received for her ninth birthday. She used her great grandmother's silver and her mother's china. The tablecloth was made in Scotland and given to Gracie's grandmother by her grandmother's sister who lived in Scotland. The furniture was brought over from Scotland by Aunt Gracie's great-grandparents.

After Uncle Gordie's death, Aunt Gracie began to take saving to new heights and started keeping empty cat food tins and jars of every conceivable type. She saved ties from bread wrappers, there were hundreds in her drawers, and there were thousands of buttons from who knew where. When she took something out of a plastic bag, she washed it and reused it until it was shredded. When Aunt Gracie died at 96, her kids pulled down trunk after trunk from the attic. Old fox stoles, shoes from the turn of the century, pictures in frames that no one could identify, wedding clothes, books, more letters, Uncle Gordie's military uniform, children's toys, and as much as several generations of a family could cram into one place. It took months to sort it all out.

Uncle Angus, who emigrated from Scotland in his 20's, married a woman from Quebec, Antoinette. While it was clear that they loved each other very much, they argued often and loud. My uncle still spoke the dying language of Scot's Gaelic, especially when he was angry, and my aunt spoke French when she was angry. Their own children used to say that they stayed together because he didn't know French and she didn't know Gaelic.

Uncle Angus and Aunt Annie, as we called her, had 13 children and named them alphabetically, Andy, Brian, Chris, Dave, Eddy, Frances, Grace, Harry, Irene, Jack, Kenny, Larry, and Matt. No one ever teased my aunt, maybe out of respect or fear, but my uncle was not spared.

"Why did he stop at M, why didn't he complete the alphabet?"

"Did he know he had a baker's dozen?"

Two things were obvious: That he had a terrific sense of humor, and they didn't believe in birth control. It was rumored that my aunt refused to leave the delivery room table after Matt was born until they tied her tubes! Who could blame her? She had completed 117 months of pregnancy!

My cousins, Fran, Gracie, and Irene, were three sisters in a family of ten brothers. As far as I could see, living with ten brothers meant automatic sainthood. I was one of three sisters also, but the ten brothers, I just couldn't fathom. I had two and they were challenging sometimes. With ten brothers, I might have turned myself over to the convent, regardless of the fact that I was Jewish.

Irene eventually did become a nun. Gracie studied to become a nun, but the urge to procreate overtook when she met the love of her life. They had eight kids. Kenny, Gracie's younger brother, was a Star Trek fan and had a very ritualized way of saying good bye to her; he would hug her, stand back, and give Spock's hand sign while reciting "live long and procreate," and it would elicit uproarious laughter from the group and smiles from Gracie. By the time I was in my 20's, Uncle Angus and Aunt Annie had 58 grandchildren and 23 great grandchildren and five great-great-grandchildren; Gracie being one of the main contributors to the family line!

While the kids of Uncle Angus and Aunt Annie grew up in shifts, the house always seemed overrun with children. Friends and cousins, including myself, were constantly going in and out.

It was not unusual for several of us to run into the house with my uncle, looking up from his newspaper inquiring, "Do ye live here?"

Someone, not necessarily his child, would answer, "Yes!" and he would go back to his reading while we giggled our way upstairs.

With that many kids outnumbering the adults, there was bound to be a little messing with the adult mind when it was already a bit challenged. When I was about eight, a group of us headed over to an uncle's cellar. This particular uncle worked in a distillery and would sometimes bring home the dregs of a rum barrel – the "spicy" sediment that drifted to the bottom of the barrel. With this, he would mix his own "home brew" and the result was called "screech."

Curious about its name and spurred on by my older cousins, we younger ones decided to taste the stuff only because our older cousins said it was ok. My cousin Peter siphoned some out of the barrel, we drank, we got silly, we drank and got sick, and then we got sick again and stayed that way for a very long time. When my aunt and uncle returned, there was hell to pay, more hell to pay when each child went home, and then more hell to pay when everyone felt better. Even at eight, it was abundantly clear to me where the stuff got its name. If you weren't screeching from its effects on your body, you were from the penance you had to pay from the adults.

With each summer that passed, the mischief became greater. A child covered in poison ivy was run of the mill. My cousins, Pete and Kenny, riding their bikes off the roof of the boathouse into the river was a small adventure that their parents eventually put an end to. If a couple of kids could get the ladder out of the barn and not be spotted by an adult, cousin Kenny would set it in place outside their bedroom window. We would climb out the second story window, running back through the house to climb out and run through again, passing by the aunts and uncles several times, scratching their heads before they put a stop to it. But when Brian and Dave decided they were going to teach us all how to water-ski, when clearly *they* didn't know how, it got a little interesting. They had everyone start from standing position on rocks. When Matt and I, the youngest kids there, decided we wanted to learn, too, they figured the rocks were too difficult, and besides, they were shredding the skis off those darn rocks. We were instructed to sit on the dock while the boat took off. The quick exit of our butts and legs over the rough wood of the dock is a memory that lives painfully on. Matt and I were flat on our stomachs for hours while sliver after sliver was removed; there were hundreds between us.

On a hot afternoon, Matt and I wanted to go for a boat ride but were too young to take the boat out on our own. Larry was not. He maneuvered the aluminum motorboat with ease, and we probably would have been fine if he hadn't met up with a friend who wanted to race. Matt and I thought it was great fun, until out of nowhere, the boat hit one of those rocks that lay only just beneath the surface. Bouncing along at a hefty clip, that boat hit the rock with such force, it sent Matt and I flying. The only reason that Larry remained in the boat was simply because he was holding onto the steering handle, but the motor had stalled on impact. Matt and I were fine, we swam back to the boat, but Larry, though sitting upright and disheveled, seemed incoherent and unresponsive, mouth agape, staring wide-eyed at a huge round rock impression in the bottom of the boat and a small but definite gap in the aluminum.

Larry's friend took us all home, with Matt repeating, "You're going to get it, Larry." And indeed, there were many Gaelic and French explicatives for days to come. I don't remember seeing much of Larry that summer, but his wide-eyed, fearful expression as his father saw us being towed home is something that is hard to forget.

In July, most of the family came to the Outlet to watch fireworks. Unlike New York State, Canada sold them freely. It wasn't unusual to have a pretty fantastic show right in the yard. We got sparklers and firecrackers by the gross. Away from the adults, I wanted to be thought of as one of the boys. They held a contest to see how long one could hold the firecrackers before they went off. As I think about this time, I marvel that no one lost a hand or an eye. We would swing strings of lit firecrackers around and let go before the last one exploded. I was so intent on keeping up with the boys that, by accident, I let one go off in my hand. My skull shook violently. It really was a stupid display of prowess for the boys. My male cousins loved me because I didn't "behave like a girl." After the last round of firecrackers, I decided I'd had enough of trying to empress the boys. When I realized I still had all my fingers, I decided I had entertained my cousins enough for one night!

I walked up to the trailer and threw myself on the bed and listened to fireworks going off, freighters long shrill whistles and cruise ship's deep throaty bellows in the shipping channel. It was late and most of the adults had gone to bed; I could hear my cousins talking low so as not to disturb the adults. After a few minutes, all the kids were called inside by their parents. I squeezed my fingers, they hurt. I fell asleep in my clothes.

Chapter Ten

Wombat Dreams

*1*982 was a busy year. I graduated from San Francisco State in mid-May. I had a part-time job in Pediatric Cardiology that had put me through school, and now that I'd graduated, they wanted me full-time. The first Gay Games were to take place at Kezar Stadium in San Francisco on September 5th. My oldest brother and his wife were having their third child in September. I started looking for a house I could afford in the Bay Area and I was flying back to New York State in early June for the annual June gathering. June was the month of my parent's anniversary. This year, it would be their 34th. It was also Father's Day, my dad's birthday, and the month the kids got out of school for the summer.

Kate, my oldest and dearest friend, would be flying in from Ghent, Belgium, where she had just graduated from the university with her Masters in Psychology. She was staying at my parent's home with me to attend the wedding of our very good friends. Terry and Charlie, who would be married on Saturday, June 5th. Terry was a good friend who grew up across the street from me and Charlie was a guy I used to work with, who became a very close friend.

In late October of 1982, I was taking a two-month trip to Australia with a friend. Charlie, Terry, Kate, my traveling companion, Kat and I agreed to meet on Saturday, October 23rd to say good bye because we didn't know when we would see each other again. Charlie and Terry were moving from New Jersey to Tacoma, Washington. Kate was taking time after graduation to travel and see her family and friends over the course of a month.

The cab pulled into my parent's driveway and my youngest sister came running out of the house, dragging Kate with her. Kate was laughing and so was I, watching the two of them.

"We have to go pick up Mom and Dad's anniversary cake," said Julia.

"First, I need to get inside and say hello to everyone. Who's here, Julia?" I paid the cabby, he had already pulled my bags out.

"Jack came over, and Barb is here with the girls. She is due to deliver in mid-September."

"I know! Joan is here, she's ready to deliver any minute."

My sister Joan came from North Carolina to stay with my parents after her husband, in the military, was shipped overseas. She was about one month away from delivering her first child. Julia and I hugged and she took off into the house. Kate said hello and we hugged and kissed. "How was your flight?" I asked.

"Long," she said and smiled.

"When did you get in?" I inquired.

"Yesterday evening." Kate took one of my bags and I carried the other.

"I've missed you," I said.

"I've missed you, too," said Kate. I looked at her and smiled. She was as relaxed as I had seen her in years. She was decked out in a pair of plaid shorts, flip flops, and a bright blue T shirt. "I wish I was going with you," Kate remarked. She gave me a little sideways nudge. "I have a surprise for you, Jan."

"You do? Tell me, Kate, how does it feel to be back in your quaint neighborhood?"

"It just feels comforting and somewhat humbling."

"I know what you mean. Those are some cute shorts," I said.

"They're Mindy's, I sort of stole them."

"You've been to Quincy already then?"

"Yes, I spent five days with my father, his wife, Julie and Mindy."

"How are they doing?"

"Mindy is about to finish nursing school in January. I think she wants to stay in Quincy and work at one of the local clinics. She feels they need the help and she's had ideas for a long time about how to improve things there. That's Mindy, you know, Jan, always the humanitarian." We walked in and I said hello to everyone.

After about half an hour of talking and coffee, Joan got up and stretched.

"Where are you off to?" Mom wanted to know.

"We have an errand to run," said Joan. Joan, Julia, Kate, and I drove to Graziano's Bakery and picked up Mom and Dad's anniversary cake All of us were going to take them to out to dinner at the Beaches Restaurant, one of Rome's finest, then come home and have some cake and coffee with their best friends, Fred and Bertie. Kate took a sip of her coffee.

"So, Virginia, to what do you attribute 34 wonderful years?" she asked.

"Lots of hard work and love." Everyone smiled. "How about you, Jake."

"I give my wife anything she wants, tell her she's the most beautiful woman in the world and... I tell her she is always right!" We laughed.

My mother's response was "He has me confused with his girlfriend!" We all cracked up. My father was still laughing when Joan went to the kitchen to make another pot of coffee. After a few minutes, she came back with a full carafe of coffee.

"Ok, we're off," she said, and the four of us walked out to the car.

By the time we got back home, Mom and Dad were relaxing outside. My sister put the cake in the garage on an old kitchen chair. Everyone was having a good time as I watched them play ping pong. I was headed inside to sort out the contents of my suitcase. Kate followed me in. My parents had given Kate and I the largest room at the back of the house. It overlooked the back yard. Kate hurried ahead of me and closed the curtains and one of the windows. I softly closed and locked the bedroom door. Kate was standing in back of me when I turned around. Our lips met and she put her hand on the middle of my back and pulled me to her. I reached for the button on her shorts. We kissed for a really long time, each pulling the other still closer.

"God I've missed you, Kate."

"Um," was all she said and I reached for the zipper on her shorts.

"Wait," Kate said. "I have a surprise for you."

"What!" I said emphatically.

"This way," and she pulled me to the bedroom door. Just then, we heard my mother and brother move from the yard to the garage to play ping pong. We waited until we heard them all in the garage.

"Come on," Kate said softly. "Now close your eyes and hold on to me."

She led me to the back yard and stopped, "Now open your eyes." There on the far side of the lawn was the old tent we slept in as kids! We both laughed and hugged each other.

"Oh, Kate, it's a wonderful surprise! I guess kids are still putting tents up in the summer to sleep outside," I said.

"And learning to spark!" whispered Kate. We both laughed. "Come," she said, "I've furnished it." She unzipped the door. "Tonight, we are slipping out here to have some 'fun,'" said Kate as she smiled a very sexy smile. Fun was the word we used as kids when we wanted to have sex. Suddenly, I felt kind of like a kid, complete with fear of being found out! I hadn't told my parents about Kate and I. I was sure, as were my sibs, that my father knew, and he had no worries about it, but I wasn't too sure my mother would be ok with it.

As Kate and I walked into the garage, my father turned and said, "Come on, Jan. Julia isn't much of a challenge!"

"Hey… that's not fair, Dad."

"Go stand with your father, Julia and Jan and I will play you both," Kate said. She paired up with Dad and the four of us had a pretty good game. The weather was cooling off, but it had been a day in the 90's and playing a vigorous game of ping pong in the high humidity and decreasing heat was not the way to cool off. My father wiped his brow, then sat down on the same chair the anniversary cake was resting on.

"DAD!" we all yelled in unison. Kate and I took the cake inside to see if we could repair it, but no, it looked bad.

"What will we tell Fred and Bertie?" Julia asked.

"We'll tell them it's Dad's ass print!" said Joan. Fortunately, it tasted delicious.

On Saturday, the 5th of June, our dear friends, Charlie, Terry, all of their family, friends gathered at St. Peter's Church in Rome, NY. They stood up in front of us all and proclaimed their love for each other. It was beautiful. Terry looked so incredibly gorgeous and looked for all the world like she was floating down the aisle on her father's arm. Everyone stood, just riveted on her. Her youngest brothers were laughing about something. Then my eyes went to Charlie. He was smiling, but his eyes were glistening.

Kate leaned over and whispered, "He's crying, Jan" and indeed he was.

He'd been through a lot in the last three years since Krisi's death. Her death had pretty much wrecked him. We were all concerned that he was so down for so long. When I introduced Charlie to Terry in January of this year, his whole countenance changed. His handsome face lit up. With a sigh of relief, we had Charlie back again. It had taken them five months to fall madly in love and tie the knot. Terry was almost three months pregnant with their first daughter, who they planned to name Anne after her mother. But that news was to be kept quiet because John and Anne Ricci were devout Catholics, going to church every day. John was also the head of the Right to Life Movement, Central New York State Chapter, and had on more than one occasion chained himself to the local women's clinic. His newest tactic was to get a gallon or so of blood from the butcher and douse himself and anyone with him with it while chained to the clinic gate. He was rabid and just a little scary when he was fired up. Anne and John had raised nine kids and he exacted ridged behavior from his kids, especially the boys. Any evening in the summer, one of his sons could be seen banging threw the screen door with John, belt in hand, in hot pursuit. One night my father and I were sitting out front and witnessed the above scenario, except that John slipped on the wet grass and went down on his can. My father roared with laughter.

Last year I started to look around for a traveling buddy for my Australia trip. I asked Kate, but she couldn't go because she planned to visit with her family for a month or longer. So, I talked to another friend, Kat. She expressed interest in going. She thought about it for a couple of days and then called back to say she would go. Kat was introduced to me by Kate. In the late 70's, I was on vacation in Boston with Kate. She told me about a woman she met just recently, Kat, who was a forest ranger. She taught Kate to wind surf, and Kat was quite good at it, jumping the waves and launching herself way up and over.

Kat was famous, apparently, but I didn't know that then. When I first met her, she told me that she had a huge party on her birthday. She said that the day of her birthday, she rented two hotel rooms for an afternoon and invited her friends and anyone they wanted to bring. The doors connecting the rooms were opened and one could go back and forth, having as much sex with whomever you chose. There were only two rules. They were to keep the noise down and NO MEN! Kat asked me once if I would like to join her for her birthday. I declined. It never occurred to me that Kate was going to them. Kate was shocked when I told her that Kat, the forest ranger, was going to join me in my trip to Australia.

I'd always wanted to go to the Land Down Under. I first became captivated with the country when I was a small child and the Sunday night kids show "Lassie" ended their run with Timmy and family having to give up Lassie because they were moving to Australia, and since Australia had quite a long quarantine period, they opted not to take their pet. As a teenager, I started reading about Australia and learned it started as a penal colony of England. England had laws in place that were barbaric. You could be shipped off to Australia if you were 7 or 70, if you were man or woman for offences, such as stealing a loaf of bread. Consequently, England's jails became so over crowded that they had to find another place to house them. At first, America offered them a solution for a penal colony, but that quickly changed when they discovered Australia. I eventually found the book, Fatal Shore, about the whole process of becoming a penal colony. I was intrigued by the history. I read every book I could get my hands on about the Land Down Under. While I was fascinated with Australia's history, I learned quickly that Aussies were not. Thinking that your ancestors were thieves and such is not something they treasure.

My cousin Rick had recently moved to California from Chicago and we became very close. He was working as an ER nurse at San Francisco General. I asked him to stay at my apartment and make it look lived in while I took my trip. Rick was happy to oblige. I knew each time he had been there because he always left a joint in a glass test tube on the bedside stand.

Kat came out on the 22nd of October to meet up with Kate, Charlie, Terry and I before everyone took off in different directions. We wouldn't see each other until well into next year. Everyone met at my place. We caught each other up on news and had a few laughs. Charlie and Terry were settled in Tacoma with their first child, Anne. Anne was born in early September. When they tried to tell her parents, John and Anne Ricci, that the baby was premature, they insisted on coming to Tacoma. Fortunately, Ellen, Terry's sister, intervened and said she would fly up and spend time with Terry.

"Tragedy averted," said Charlie.

"Would they have really created a ruckus?" asked Kat. In unison, we shook our heads and replied in the affirmative that John would have. "Good grief," said Kat.

"My father would never have talked to either of us again," said Terry.

On October 28th, Kat and I left SFO for Sydney by way of New Zealand. On arrival, everyone was chomping at the bit after 16 hours of flight, but we were told to stay in our seats as the New Zealand Health Officers came through spraying the air over us. Before too long, we were landing in Sydney. After a tiring trip through customs, collecting the bags, and renting a car, we drove to a hotel, an easy venture one might think, but not so, for Aussies drive on the left side of the road. The steering wheel is on the right and the stick-shift is on the left. This is all backwards for us yanks.

We checked into the hotel overlooking Bondi Beach. We were on the top floor of the hotel and could see the partially nude bathers. Some of the beaches in Australia are nude but most are topless. They are a country relaxed about their bodies. I went in the bathroom and ran the water at the sink. When I was a kid, I read about Australia and found that because it is under the equator, the water turns in the opposite direction when there is a whirlpool; it was true, it did.

I needed a nap, so I got undressed and laid down. I woke about super time and my companion, Kat, was nowhere to be found. Moments later, she burst in.

"Hey, I met some dykes. Let's get something to eat."

I pulled on my clothes and we found a restaurant downstairs. One of the first things we learned about this country was that their time frame for meals is much different than ours is. While we might take an hour or hour and a half for a meal, it is not unusual for Aussies to take two or three hours for a meal.

After our repast, we drove to the far side of Sydney to visit some friends. On the way there, Kat told me about the lesbians she met. Clearly, she was excited to find fellow "bowlers" so far from home. The neighborhoods in Sydney didn't look too much different from what you would see at home. We rang the bell and waited. Mark, Julie, and son David came screaming out of the front door. "You made it," Julie exclaimed, "David, you are at least a foot taller than I remember!"

"Oh gosh, you aren't going to start pinching my cheeks; are you? My grandmother follows with the cheek pinching when she tells me how much I've grown! No cheek pinching here, mate." "You're catching on to the lingo," said David. "Come on in."

We all went into the house amidst hugs and excited chatter.

"We really like it here," said Mark, "but we don't get many visitors from the Bay Area."

Julie had worked at BART, which is where she met Mark. They worked for a time together before coming back to Julie's home and family in Sydney.

"How does it feel to be out of BART, you two?" BART stood for Bay Area Rapid Transit. Mark worked there since its inception in San Francisco in the early 70's. By the time I met Mark and Julie, David was about ten. We'd get together at the Marina, bring a picnic, and take advantage of the gusty winds there to fly kites.

We shared some drinks and laughter and caught both of them up to date on everyone they left behind.

"It's a long flight to get here," Kat said. Mark looked up from his glass "It took us 16 hours in the air," Kat enumerated.

"That's precisely why we don't get too many visitors from San Francisco. It's not so easy to hop on a plane and fly here," said Mark. David got up from the floor and bid everyone good night. "My last two weeks of school and I've got a ton of stuff to do."

"Summer vacation?" I said.

"Right" said David.

"Does that feel weird to have summer in what used to be your winter in the northern hemisphere?"

"Nah, I'm used to it now."

"Kids adjust fast to big changes," said Mark. We nodded in agreement. David turned around before leaving the room and said, "You might wake up early, we have big, noisy birds. It sounds like a jungle every morning." We stayed up talking until late, discussing everything from restaurants, to Mark's parents, who moved to Australia when Mark and Julie did. Mark is an only child and his parents were not about to lose their only child to another continent on the far side of the world. His parents made the trip over and purchased a house in Sydney, not too far from their only grandchild.

Mark disappeared momentarily and returned carrying a tray with crackers and cheese, a carafe of some punch and some beer.

"It's very late, why not stay over?" said Julie.

"We don't want to put you out," I said.

"Listen, you are not putting us out. We'd enjoy your company at break-fast," said Mark. We decided to stay. "One thing though, not to alarm you, but we have big spiders here. They are called Hunter spiders. They have fangs that can bite through your big toenail, they're poisonous, and they travel in pairs. The thing is, we saw one coming down the drain pipe outside the kitchen window, but we haven't found the second one yet., so be sure to check your bed and shoes before you put them on."

"Ok."

I tried not to look freaked out, but when we got in the room, I tore that bed apart, checked the floor, closet, the bathroom, and Kat's bed and then checked everything again, though no second spider was ever found!

We planned on staying in Sydney for a day or two before beginning our trek across Australia. We started the day by visiting Sydney Harbor Bridge. It's a cool looking bridge. We went shopping for clothes and food and had a picnic in a local park. We went to a book store and took in downtown. The time we spent in Sydney was too short a time to really do Sydney justice, but we would come back to it two more times before the end of our trip. Lastly, before we started our trek across the country, we wanted to see The Opera House. The Sydney Opera House is known around the world as an architec-tural marvel and is really quite beautiful on the inside and out. The outside is made to look like a ship with full sails. At the end of our trip to Australia, we would spend an evening watching "The Nutcracker." Our plan now though, was to get on the road. We would drive across the country to see as much as we could in the two months we allotted ourselves.

On the third day of our stay in Sydney, we rose early, bought some food, packed the car with about five gallons of water and an extra can of gas, and left town about 7 AM. From Sydney, we drove through the town of Wollon-gong and 178 miles to Canberra, Australia's capital, the most sterile city I think I've ever seen. There wasn't much fun to be had there. We watched a cricket game at a sports bar, trying to figure out the game without any luck, and went shopping. One day was enough to take in Canberra. The next morning, we were on the road driving the 290 miles from Canberra to Melbourne.

Melbourne, unlike Canberra, is a bustling place. It's known as Australia's unofficial sports capital. We arrived in late afternoon and headed to the central business district to look around and scope out a place to eat. Fun facts about Melbourne are that its population is about 4 million and its sister city in the U.S. is Boston. Melbourne was the first city in the state of Victoria. Sydney and Wollongong are in the state of New South Wales.

Melbourne is the fox capital of Australia, with between 6-23 foxes per square kilometer in the metropolitan area. It was also the second most populous metropolitan/urban area in Australia in 1982 but today is the largest, with almost five million people. The Australian Open happens in Melbourne in January.

A strange yet beautiful sight we witnessed was when the sun was setting and the sky was alight with beautiful oranges and reds, more than 60,000 bats, or flying foxes as the Aussies call them, come out to feed! The massive flock aims right for the skyline. They make their way from Yarra Bend Park to Melbourne's central business district. It's quite a sight to see.

Every year, Melbourne hosts the Formula 1 Grand Prix in Albert Park. The record for speed was 312 kilometers per hour, which calculates out to 193.87 miles per hour. While we hoped we could catch that, it happened during their winter, which was July and August. We arrived at the beginning of their summer in November.

The following morning, Kat and I decided to tour down town by tram and see what we could find. What we found were two lesbian couples. We struck up a conversation with the women on the tram. They were on their way to the Luna amusement park in St. Kilda. They had a roller coaster there that was the oldest continuously run roller coaster in the world, operating since 1911. We had no solid plans for the day, so when they asked us to join them, we agreed.

We ended up spending the evening together as well. After a three-hour dinner with drinks and lots of conversation, they invited us to a lesbian bar in town. Kat and I accompanied Phillipa to the bar, where she ordered six "wet pussies" for us. Kat looked at me and I at her.

"Are they drinks, Phillipa, or women," Kat asked, looking really intrigued.

"We get them every time we come here," said Phillipa.

I leaned into Phillipa, and said, "You Aussies are way more advanced than we are."

Our new friends laughed uproariously. In their wonderful accent, they explained that it was a drink of vodka and KJ peach schnapps with cranberry juice and a drop of lime. I breathed a sigh of relief and settled in to listen to the music. The dykes down under didn't look too much different than the dykes in the Bay Area, they certainly had a good sense of humor, they just sounded different.

The following morning, we met our new friends for breakfast at the Grain Store. Nora, Philippa, Ruthie, and Charlene treated us to a taste of Vegemite. They were a good group of women. They were as curious about the U.S. as we were about their island continent. As much as we wanted to continue to hang with our new friends, we felt we should continue-on, we had a lot of driving to do. We were ultimately headed to Perth, at the very southwestern tip of the country. Our next stop though was Adelaide and the Barossa Valley. Charlene and Ruthie were looking for some transportation to the Barossa Valley, which is comparable to our Napa Valley. We offered to take them as far as Adelaide. The Barossa Valley was just an hour or so beyond, and they gladly took up our offer. It was good to have another couple of drivers.

We were leaving the state of Victoria and entering the state of "South Australia." Adelaide was about 452 miles from Melbourne. If we hadn't already gotten a taste of driving in a very deserted environment, we were about to on this trip. On the stretch of road from Geelong to Adelaide, we saw some truckers and only a handful of cars. Signs were posted about the last stops for gas or water for so many kilometers, and people paid close attention to those signs. In addition, there were areas where breaks from the sun were built and water was an emergency supply. It was on this stretch of road that Charlene explained what the racks on the front of the trucks were.

"They're called roo racks."

"Roo racks," Kat echoed.

"Yes, this country has huge trucking industry and they need to move quickly through the outback, so they put these racks on the front of their trucks and they plow across the outback and if roos get in their way, as they do, then the drivers don't stop."

"That's awful," said Kat. It explained why we were seeing dead roos alongside the road.

We were really enjoying the trip with our new friends.

"Hey, Charlene and Ruthie, are you sure you don't want to make the drive to Perth with us?" said Kat.

"We'd like that, but Ruthie is meeting her mum and dad in Barossa. Hitching a ride with you has saved a fair amount of time for us."

"Glad we could help. How will you finish the last hour to the Barossa Valley?"

"Oh, we can jump on the Adelaide Metro Rail."

We finally arrived in Adelaide about eight hours after we started driving that morning. The girls caught a train for the last 45.7 miles to the Barossa Valley. They said they would be back in Melbourne in about a week. We told them our route back across Australia would not be this one but a more northerly route. We exchanged information, and they assured us they would be making a trip to San Francisco. We said our goodbyes and watched as they approached the ticket window.

"Well then," Kat inquired, "what do you know about Adelaide, Jam?"

Her nickname for me was short for Jamboozel. The nickname came about when we threw a surprise party for a friend, Carla, and my job was to spend the day with her and make her believe that I would ultimately take her to the airport, so she could fly to LA and spend her birthday with her girlfriend, when in reality, her girlfriend was already in San Francisco with about 50 of her closest friends for a surprise party. To get her to the flat, I told her that I was to pick up something at a friend's place and we walked up together, but when the door opened, there was everyone to surprise her. Our friend Carla was totally taken off guard! Kat told everyone how successfully I had bamboozled Carla and I became (to Kat anyway) Jamboozel, shortened to "Jam." I explain that here to short circuit any ideas that it has some significant meaning or that Kat didn't know what my real name was!

In any case, Kat persisted. "So, what do you know about Adelaide?"

"Let's see, I know no convicts settled in this city."

"Really."

"Yes, really. I also know they have the oldest surviving German settlement."

"How very odd, you mean, like the Amish, speaking German and retaining their own culture?" "Yes, I believe so. And it's home to the largest display of aboriginal artifacts."

That was one of the things we hoped to see in Adelaide. The other was The Fringe Festival, which is the largest art festival in the Southern Hemisphere and second largest in the world.

"Here's an interesting tidbit, a place called Anna's Creek station, it's the largest working cattle station in the world. It used to be a sheep ranch, but dingo attacks caused them to shift their focus to cattle. At 6 million acres, it's as big as the country of Israel or as big as ten small European countries."

"WOW, got any other snippets?"

"Yup. Says here that the state of South Australia has over 1.5 million people. Over 75% live with in the metropolitan area of Adelaide. 25% of South Australia's residents were not born in Australia."

We liked Adelaide a lot and planned to stay several days and take in the sites. The first morning out, we went to the Flying Fig Deli for some boiled bagels. It was good fare. We had them wrap a couple of bagels for lunch as well. We took the Adelaide Metro Tram to take in a few sites for our first day. It was good to have a car, but we decided not to use it as much as we could. Taking the tram line made it easy to leave the car behind, and we felt unencumbered. Kat wanted to start with Adelaide Botanical Garden, where they had exotic plants. Next was my pick, and I wanted to see South Australia Museum, to take in Australia's national heritage. We went to the Art Gallery of South Australia. It's a colonnaded gallery founded in 1881. They had a park, where you could hike with kangaroos and emu's. Then we went to Cleland's Conservation Park and hiked trails with scenic vista's, stopping to ditch our boots and go for a swim in the waterfalls. On one of the last days, we went to Himeji Gardens. This was a green Japanese oasis with a beautiful lake. On the last day, we visited Tandanya National Aboriginal Museum, which was spectacular, and St. Peter's Anglican Cathedral, consecrated in 1878.

Again, we met a couple of lesbians on the tram and learned that Adelaide has long been LBGT friendly. They gave us the name of a place where lesbians hung out and that was the Wheatsheaf Hotel, open at 1 PM, a folksy bar serving regular live music events. So, we spent the day in the Barossa Valley at the Lihhans Winery and Rusden Winery, and then on our last night, went to the Wheatsheaf Hotel for some drinks and to listen to some live music. We paled around with some gals we met there but said our goodbyes and went back to the hotel to get some shut-eye so we could leave in the morning. We had a busy and enjoyable week in Adelaide.

The next morning, we rose and slogged to the café for some breakfast. Hungover is what we were from all the alcohol the day before, from sun up to sun down. Today, we were going to make our way to Coober Pedy. While Adelaide was the opal capital of Australia, Coober Pedy is where the sweat was. In the unbearably hot and dusty outback lay the little town where its residents lived underground.

Coober Pedy's mines more than 80% of the world's opals. This town is squarely in the middle of the hot Australian outback. The people who live here live below ground in caves called dugouts, which are built, or rather carved out, because of the scorching heat during the day. In the mining town of Coober Pedy, temperatures in the outback can reach 50 Celsius or 122 degrees.

The first thing Kat and I did after we arrived was to scope-out our underground hotel and rest a bit from the heat. When we finally rose from our nap, we were anxious to search out what we came for: Opals!

Umoona Opal Mine and Museum, is the largest single underground tourist attraction. Neither it nor the rest of the town look like any living thing is there, but once you go underground, their world opens up to you.

Later in the day, as the sun was setting, we took a drive on the surface to Stuart Street in Coober Pedy. What we found there was Australia's Dog Fence. It was listed in the tourist info, so we figured it was worth a look. If there is one thing you can say about Aussies, they do things in a big way, and this was just another example. It was a pet exclusion fence to keep dingoes (wild dogs) away from sheep, which was and is a huge industry. Before the dog fence, one sheep station (ranch), many of which are massive (as big as small countries), lost 11,000 sheep in a year to dingoes. Another station lost 3,000 to dingoes. The dog fence is 2,225 km long or 1,383 miles long. The fence was started in the 1800's and maintenance continues to this day.

The last place we visited was a dug-out called Crocodile Harry's. This place was way out of the way and difficult to get to, but we both thought it was worth the effort. It was called the Playboy Mansion of the Outback, and the guy who created it had a life that made the guy in Crocodile Dundee pale in comparison, although the character of Crocodile Dundee was based on his life.

The following morning after purchasing our weight in Opals, we left Coober Pedy, and as much as I liked the people and town, I was not sorry to leave the heat behind.

From Coober Pedy, we decided to backtrack to get to the main highway; again, it meant several hours of driving, but we did it for safety. Although there were country roads, they weren't as well maintained as the main highway. In other words, there weren't signs telling you how far to the next gas or the next water or rest stop with a barrier from the sun, and since we were novices at traveling in the outback, we needed all the help we could get. "Coober Pedy to Ceduna is 1,003 km or 10 hours driving." The main road, Eyre's Highway, had a handful of small towns and a couple of places that said they were towns but consisted of only a couple of houses.

When we got back on Eyre's Highway, we were near the town of Ceduna, where we called it a day.

"Just an FYI, did you know that the longest golf course starts in Ceduna."

"No kidding. I had no idea!" I said to Kat.

"It's called the Nullarbor Links Golf Course. The 18th hole is 1,365 kilometers away at Kalgoorlie."

"That's one long golf game."

The Nullarbor Plain and the heat combined with slightly over ten hours of driving left us completely exhausted and just a little punchy. We got a room and laid down for the night. The morning found us hungry and pouring over maps.

"We're getting over run with maps," said Kat, holding several maps out to me.

"I'm kind of thinking that I might just keep them, so I remember distances and such."

"Ok" and she set them down. We looked at the places we had yet to reach.

"We have about 5 1/2 hours tomorrow to reach Eucla, we can stop or keep going and just pull over somewhere and sleep." Kat looked at me like I'd lost my mind.

"Are you crazy?" I knew full well that she wouldn't agree to not getting a decent night's sleep. "Ok, ok, I'll indulge your extravagant behavior."

"On to Eucla!"

Eucla would be a small milestone as we crossed into another state, Western Australia.

We pulled into a gas station to tank up the car and get some stuff to throw in the cooler. While Kat was pumping the gas, I wandered outside to the back of the store/gas station. There was an old telegraph station whose roof had blown off but whose walls stood yet. I took my shoes off, because they would fill with sand, and I carried them. As I climbed to the top of the wall and stood there, looking down into the heart of the old building, suddenly, I heard someone yelling and turned around to see the owner waving and yelling at me. At first, I thought something had happened to Kat. The man was frantic.

"Come down from there. Hurry, come down."

I did, then looked at him as though he had a few screws loose. "You can't go on the sand. There are snakes in the sand, and when you walk on the surface, they feel the vibration and think they have dinner. The snakes here are very poisonous and we have no anti venom, so if you get bitten, you will die within about 15 minutes."

That was a sobering thought, I tucked it away in my brain. Somebody was looking out for me. Kat rounded the corner.

"What's all the yelling about?"

"Nothing, I'll tell you later."

We spent one day and night driving The Great Australian Bight.

"Why do they call it that?"

"I think because of its shape."

"Oh hmm," said Kat.

"They're very literal."

"Well, and so what about the Nullarbor Plain? That sounds like an aboriginal name."

I just laughed. "The name has more to do with Latin than with the aboriginals."

Kat looked at the name again and said, "Oh, no trees."

"Righto, missy," I said, smiling. A treeless plain and indeed it was. There were no trees for miles and miles, and by the time we finished driving the Nullarbor, it would be hundreds of miles. There were only low shrubs, no taller than your knees.

"I read information about the Nullarbor," I said to Kat, "and it said that in the 1950's, the Nullarbor was used for British atomic and nuclear testing."

"Really, is it still radioactive? Will we light up when we fly back home?" We both laughed rather nervously.

"I'm sure it must have been under ground. The Nullarbor is a pretty huge place."

The land was so vast that one could clearly see the curvature of the earth.

"Did you know, Jan, where ever you see the earth curve that you've just ticked off four miles?" "I did know that actually."

Kat liked history and trivia, like me. We decided to take a detour. We wanted to see the abandoned Koonalda homestead. The homestead used to be a train station, functional during the mid-1900's. It was a stop-over for folks on a journey across the Nullarbor, via Eyre's Highway. There was an old sheering shed with tools still hanging on the wall. It was also a stopover for those looking for fuel or food. A field accommodated what is known as the car graveyard. The graveyard had a motley collection of old cars, abandoned, in various stages of decay.

Fifteen km past the homestead, we learned of an array of caverns and sink holes. We couldn't leave that area without seeing this. These caves and sink holes have been the topic of interest for cavers and explorers for a while. This cave system is known around the world for being some of the most intensive systems discovered yet. We were not disappointed, even though it delayed us a couple of hours.

The next morning, we got up early and made the decision to try and make it to Kalgoorlie, which meant 13 hours of driving or 699 miles. We spent time trying to entertain each other because the drive was so monotonous. We sang Australian children's songs:

> "Kookaburra sits on the old gum tree
> Merry merry king of the bush is he…" or
> Waltzing Matilda, waltzing Matilda,
> Who'll come a waltzing Matilda with me….

Whenever I traveled, I picked up a children's books from the local stores. I bought one at every stop in Australia. So, we read them to one another as part of our entertainment. There were some really good ones. My favorite was a story about a little boy whose stuffed bear comes to life at night, and they dig a hole from England to Australia and go on various adventures by sliding down the tunnel they made and climbing back up to get back home to England. Their adventures included the Outback or watching the penguins or going to the Barrier Reef. Then we had a book of Australian children songs and nursery rhymes.

We played games as well.

"Ok, let's have a rousing game of believe it or not," Kat said as she drove.

"You go first," I said.

"Name three things that have been physically difficult."

"Let me see, jumping out of an airplane, being in the army, and breaking my leg skiing."

"You jumped out of an airplane? When did you do that? I didn't know you were in the army. When was that? And you broke your leg, how long ago?"

"Aren't we playing a game here? You're supposed to guess which is true and which is a lie," said Kat.

"Oh, right, well, the part about being in the military."

"That's correct. Your turn."

"Wait just a minute, 'splain about the broken leg and jumping out of an airplane."

"About 12th grade, I went skiing at Killington, Vermont and was showing off, fell, and broke my leg."

"What on earth were you doing?" Kat rolled her eyes.

"Are you playing this game with me or not?"

"Ok, new question though. I don't want to think about being through some very painful things." Kat rolled her eyes again. "Ok, name three things in life you would repeat."

"Oh, that's easy, the summer after 6th grade, the summer after 10th grade, and going to Kate's graduation from Brown." Something tells me that all those are true and they all involve Kate. I felt a little like a school girl with a crush, thinking about Kate. We decided to listen to music.

Occasionally, we would see a dead kangaroo. This particular day, we saw a herd of camels. There must have been close to a dozen.

"They brought these girls over from the Middle East," said Kat.

"Yes, they're imported from Afghanistan, Arabia, and India. They were used for transport and heavy work. When the car came along, they were no longer needed, so several thousands were released into the wild."

Later that day, we would spot several Emus, an ostrich looking creature, and as we drove past them, they acted as though we were challenging them to a race and started running along-side the car. It was pretty funny. One other thing of notice were the magpies and crows who would stand on the side of the road and wait for a vehicle to runover and kill bugs for them to eat. Anywhere there were sheep grazing, the magpies would imitate the bleating of the sheep. It happened where ever you saw sheep and sometimes where you didn't. The birds just learned to make the noise the sheep would make and imitate each other's sounds.

Other things that made us laugh were Aussie road signs, like a picture of koala or wombat crossing sign on the road or picture of a camel for a camel crossing or platypus crossing. One thing that really cracked us up was the sayings for different states, and what they called the folks who lived in those states. People in New South Wales are called Cockroaches, those who live in Queensland are referred to as Banana-benders, folks in south Australia are known as Crow-eaters, people in Tasmania are Tassies, folks in Victoria are Gum-Suckers, and the residents of Western Australia are called Sand-Gropers. Western Australia is also known as the state of excitement!

When darkness fell, we were treated to the most incredible sky. Because we were in the middle of the outback and there were no city lights at all within 100 miles of us. We looked up to see the sky brilliant with stars! There were so many, you'd reach the millions if you tried to count one square inch. You could read a book by the light. I don't think I ever realized just what the night sky could look like if you didn't have light from cities to diffuse the sky. We stopped the car on the shoulder, turned it off, threw a beach towel on the roof. Then we climbed up, laid down, put our heads together, and stared at the phenomenal show of lights before us. It was kind of a tender moment and Kat reached over and pulled me to her as we rested on the roof. We had the whole southern hemisphere of stars to ourselves.

We pulled into Kalgoorlie with a high expectation of getting lots of rest, a bath maybe, some good food, a beer, and a good mattress to sleep on. We got all that and more.

"Kalgoorlie is an old mining town," said Kat. "We have several things in common with the Aussies," insisted Kat.

"Do tell."

"Well, for instance, we had our gold rush in the mid 1800's and so did Australia. Also, we started as a penal colony and so did the Aussies."

"You're a wealth of information."

"Yes, I am," Kat smiled in my direction.

"Anything else?"

"Let's see what else they say here. The town was founded in 1893 during the Yilgarn Goldfields gold rush."

In the morning, we finished breakfast and went off to find the 18th hole that belonged to the longest golf course in the world. We walked in and out of shops, stopped for lunch at a little mom and pop hash house, and met a couple from a Canada. We hung out together, talking, about where we had been and where we wanted to go yet. Then Kat and I went up to our room in this very old hotel. We had a couple of Australian beers with us.

"Who is going to drive first tomorrow?" asked Kat.

"I guess I can," I said without any conviction.

Kat put a cassette in the player we brought. She grabbed the church key from the counter and tossed it to me for the bottles of beer. Then she threw her body on the bed next to me.

"Is this trip everything you'd hoped it might be?"

"It's pretty close," I said.

"I was surprised that you called to ask me to go with you."

"Why were you surprised? You and I talked about going."

"Yeah, I know, but you and Kate were together every time I saw you, so I thought you were partners." I sat quietly for moment.

"Yes, we are and we aren't."

"What does that mean?"

"Kate is studying in Europe, and I live in Northern California. We don't see each other enough to be considered a couple. However, when we do get together, it's as if we were never apart."

"I see."

"How did you and Kate meet?"

"We kind of grew up together. You've been together for a long time, haven't you?"

"Since 1968," I said.

"When did her family move from Rome?"

"They moved to Montauk, Long Island in 1969." I must have looked puzzled at her questions because she stopped asking them.

"Why are you asking all the questions?"

"Oh, I don't know, just curious, I guess." I looked at Kat and wondered if she had thought about being with me. She and I got together once when she came to Rome, but it was after Kate left for Europe and I felt then and still feel that it was because I was already missing Kate and that it was not necessarily in good taste.

We didn't want to hang out in Kalgoorlie too long because Perth was only about 6 1/2 hours away, and we were considering one more stop before we got to Perth. The next morning we took some pictures of the old hotel, gassed up the car, and hit the road.

Wave rock was our one more stop. It's 296 km or 184 miles east, southeast of Perth. It's a giant striated rock called Hyden's Rock that lies about two miles east of the small town of Hyden. Wave rock has one shear side of granite that looks like a giant wave about to break. Its 26 meters or 49 feet high, and 110 meters or 360 feet long. Wave rock was formed before the age of the dinosaurs. It's, without question, the most interesting rock I've ever seen.

Before we arrived in Perth, we saw in the distance, as we descended a hill the marina on the far side of the city. Kat was driving.

I leaned forward, "It reminds me of San Diego!" "It does kind of," said Kat. We navigated our way to Freemantle, a suburb near Perth. We rented a one-bedroom serviced apartment on the peninsula for at least a week. When we pulled into the driveway, I saw Kat' eyes light up. There were people out on the water wind surfing. She loved to wind surf and planned to in Sydney but realized she could do a lot of that here.

After we went to the office to sign papers and asked where to rent wind surfing gear, we got our bags from the car and settled in pretty quickly.

"Kat, why don't we stay here for today, so you can do some wind surfing."

"I would love that. I'll take you to dinner tomorrow night Aussie style," she said.

"Would that be new fish to try and three hours long?"

"That's right," I smiled at her.

Quite frankly, l was glad she wanted to stay here, I was excited to finally arrive in Perth, but I was exhausted after days of driving in the hot Australian outback.

"If you don't mind, while you surf, I'm going to shower and take a nap."

"That will be good to regenerate you."

So, Kat went to rent a board and I got in the shower. When I got out, I walked around with the towel, looking at the apartment, and caught sight of Kat on the water. Kate was right, she was really good. She would go up the wave and jump at the top, winding back and forth and sailing down the front. I watched her for several minutes, then laid down on the bed with the towel over me and fell into a deep sleep.

I awoke with Kat lying next to me. She was a little sun burned, smiling, and naked.

"You slept for a long time, eh? I was out with the board for 2 1/2 hours and just got back."

"Yeah, I saw you. You're very good at it."

"I've been doing it for years. Would you like me to teach you how to wind surf?"

"Sure."

I wondered why Kat hadn't made any sexual advances to me. I decided to make the first move. Kat was leaning on her elbows, looking out the window. She started to speak.

"Why don't we find some…"

I positioned myself on my elbows and gently reached over to kiss her. My kiss had short circuited her conversation. Instead, she grabbed me and kissed me back. We spent several minutes kissing and inching closer until our bodies were up against each other. My body came alive for the first time in months. I thought briefly of Kate but then didn't and became comfortable in pursuing what I knew would be the eventual outcome.

We stayed in our little apartment, paying an off-duty employee to run quickly for a few groceries for us, telling him we would pay him well.

"You know, I was feeling that I was treading on sacred ground, thinking you and Kate were perhaps exclusive."

"How would that play out?" I said as I pulled my robe on, "She's in Europe and I'm in California. We see each other maybe every eight months to a year, if we're lucky. I hardly think being exclusive to me is something she thinks about at this point in her life, maybe someday, but certainly not now." Kat grabbed me and pulled me to her. She was very strong. With that, I became totally unhinged. She took my hand and led me to the living room. She had grabbed her bathrobe on the way out of the bedroom. She put the robe on and sat on the couch. I opened my robe, then I opened hers and climbed on her lap. My breasts fell level with her mouth. Just as she leaned forward to take them, there was a knock at the door.

"Shit," said Kat. I climbed off, closed my robe, and answered the door.

Our first full-day in Perth saw us cruising around looking at everything and then we decided to take a city bus tour, and at the last minute, decided to take a cruise on the Bay. From the Bay, we visited the historic Round House Prison. By dinner-time, we were hungry, but we went home to the apartment. We planned to sit and talk about tomorrow over some supper. Instead we walked in the door and grabbed on to each other like we were struggling to stay afloat on a sinking ship and tore each other's clothes off like we were on fire!

Kat stopped, stepped back, and held her hand up in a halt position and said, "What are we doing, here?" She just brought our evening's activities to a screeching halt with five words.

"We spend weeks together and suddenly we can't stop groping each other?"

"Does this need analyzing?" I said.

"No," responded Kat.

"Well then, shut up and come over here, dammit."

"Too bad you didn't bring your forest rangers hat."

"You like uniforms then?" said Kat.

"I like them on you!" We laughed.

The following morning, we woke to sounds of birds that squawked so loud, we thought we were in a jungle. I remember David warning us about the birds in the morning. We had some tea and toast and planned the day. We started the day with the Western Australian Museum. It was spectacular! We packed a lunch, and when we finished at the museum, we drove to Yellagong Park for a picnic. We did a lot of talking about the last few days; the whole tenor of our relationship had changed.

"You know, Kat, this isn't really going to materialize into much more than a very special friendship."

"Yes, I'm aware."

"I know you are, I just wanted to say it. Massachusetts and California are not neighbors! I'm sorry if I complicated things." We brought wine and I poured some for both of us.

"It is what it is, sweetie."

"I'm kinda big on monogamy, so, Ms. Ranger, when are you ever going to be monogamous?" I teased.

"That's Ms. Park Ranger to you, and my answer to that is when I lose function of my fingers or we have no more electricity!"

"You're crazy," I said.

In the afternoon, we went to the Caversham Wildlife Park where we had some fun with the kangaroos and got to hold a koala. It was cute as it could be, but it stunk to high heaven. The beaches around Perth and Freemantle were gorgeous and we spent hours sunning. Swimming was a whole other activity here than it was at home. There were shark fences to keep sharks away from swimmers. They appeared to be working well. At Bondi Beach in Sydney, we got a chance to see one when a friend of David's took us out in a boat while he inspected the fence. He worked for New South Wales to upkeep shark fences. He told us that occasionally sharks would ram the fences, not because they wanted to break them down, but because the fence gave off a slight electrical charge and it confused them about what was there, e.g. a dying fish or something to eat.

If one was going to the beach, you were forewarned to take vinegar with you. The jelly fish were in abundance in some areas. If they were a constant threat, they would post signs. Somehow the vinegar would serve to help with the stinging burning pain. One evening after supper, Kat and I were walking barefoot on a beach while we carried our shoes. We were stopped by a young guy who was kind enough to tell us that there are fish called rock fish that were hard to tell apart from the rocks and the could give you quite a sting. They wouldn't kill you, but they would make you very sick.

We decided while we were in Perth that we would see the famous Lake Hillier on an island, two hours off the coast. Lake Hillier is known as the Pink Lake. It's fascinating to see, especially from the air. When I first saw it, I was a kid looking at a book of Australia and it was as if someone had put strawberry milk mix in the lake. We wanted to make a day of it and spend time at the beach, on the island, before going back to the mainland. We contacted a company that took tourists for plane trips. The pilot was willing to take us to tour the lake, get a bunch of pictures, go for a swim, and eat the picnic we packed. The pilot's name was Dan. He was very personable, talkative, and very funny. He was born in England, and his family moved to Sydney when he was ten. He had six sisters! He was the only boy. I couldn't imagine. We shared our picnic with him.

It was indeed pink, brilliantly pink. Flying over the lake to land near it reminded me of the picture I saw as a little kid. It was like someone had poured Pepto-Bismol in the water. Dan explained to us that the pink was caused by the presence of Algae Dunaliella Salina, which is a source of beta carotene, a food coloring agent and a source of vitamin A. The lake also contains the world's largest microalgae which is farmed commercially to create fish food. To Dan's credit, he let us stay well past what we agreed to with no extra charge.

All In all, we got to see our pink lake and made a friend in Dan, and had a few laughs as well.

When we returned to our little apartment, it was late. We planned to lay down and nap after our fun-filled day. The following day, we decided to take a trip to Rottnest Island. It was an all-day affair. So, we filled our back packs with stuff we needed and we took a ferry from Freemantle over and spent the afternoon snorkeling and riding bicycles. Kat was able to rent a wind surf board and she was in her element. She asked me if I was ready to learn; I was. At first, she had me stand with her on her board. While she stood behind me, she showed me how to catch and maneuver the wind in the sail. I was very comfortable in her arms, she was strong and confident.

The one thing about Rottnest was the flies. If you were swimming or riding a bike, you were ok. Otherwise the flies were in your face, up your nose, in your eyes or ears. The only other way to keep them at bay was to wear an Aussie straw hat with baubles hanging down, so when you moved, it kept them off your face.

After a full day trip, we went back to the apartment, thinking we would sleep, but we never did until all matters of pleasure were attended to first. I was becoming very attached to Kat in a strange sort of way. She was older than me, taller than me, and like Kate, was a formidable presence, commanding attention. Her personality reminded me of Kate, but no one could touch Kate's beauty.

"What do you think of sticking around this area a couple of days?" Kat asked.

"That's fine with me. We can site see locally."

So, we went to King's Park, The Art Gallery of Western Australia, Cottesloe and Scarborough Beaches, we took a walking tour of Perth, explored the history of Freemantle through the markets and we walked along the Swan River. All in all, we got our money's worth from Perth.

At the end of the week, I scheduled an appointment to have the car looked at. While we didn't have any problems with it, we did put it through its paces. We rented the car with the agreement that we would have unlimited mileage and could go to any state. However, I don't think they expected that we would take them literally. We were getting ready to start our return trip and we would drive through some sparsely populated areas and some desert. If something went wrong with it, then it could be dangerous. We dropped the car at the mechanic's and we walked off to look for a place to have breakfast.

We perused the street.

"What about this place?" said Kat. It was noisy and packed full of people." There's nothing that says good food like a packed house."

We walked in and tried to figure out where everyone was ordering. I accidentally bumped the woman in front of me, and she turned around to see who the clod was behind her.

"I'm so sorry. Is this the line to order?"

She smiled and said, "No worries then, yeah, you got it, mate." I smiled back.

"This your first time here, love?" she said.

"It is."

"They serve a good cupa here."

"Do they?" Suddenly, it hit me I was talking with a "bowler." (My term for a gay woman or man).

"You a Canuck then?"

"No, American." I felt stupid saying I was American. Regan was in office and I hated him. He stopped the money for AIDS research. He was not at all endearing himself to the gay and lesbian community. I turned to tell Kat and she put her mouth to my ear.

"Jan, there are all woman here. I looked around, I hadn't noticed when we came in." They were all women; fem and butch, mixes of that and just women. "I think these are all lesbians." It was 1982 and we had just walked into a coffee house, chock a block full of dykes!

We got our coffee and breakfast and went outside to the courtyard, in the back. I looked up and saw the woman I ran into earlier.

"Hello there."

"Hey, mate, I'm glad to catch you, you dropped this while you were gettin brekky." It was the mechanic's business card.

"I'd be screwed if I lost this."

"So, your car is at the servo?"

"If you mean mechanic, then yes."

"Do you Sheilas need s lift?"

"We were just going to stay in this area until we get the car, but thanks. What is your name?" "It's Lindsey."

"It's very nice to meet you. I'm Jan and this is Kat. Do you live in Perth?"

"Yes, but I'm from Tasmania."

"Really? You're a long way from home." She nodded yes.

She looked at her watch, "Crikey, I have to get going..."

"Hey, Lindsey," she had bolted for the door, but looked back at us and hesitated. "Would you like to get some tea here tomorrow morning?" She shook her head yes and waved, then took off. I stood watching her leave and realized that everyone in the place was looking at me. I sat down and Kat smiled and said, "Guess they think you have a funny accent!"

We'd picked up the car and went back to the apartment. We were going to strategize about heading back across the country, but we wanted to take a ride up north a bit. We didn't know how far.

"How about to Geraldton? That way we might be able to connect to this east/west route."

"Seems alright to me."

We didn't realize then that the connecting roads were dirt and slow going.

The following morning, we headed to the city to see if we could hook-up with Lindsey. We got our tea and scones and sat in the front window. Before too long, we saw Lindsey walking briskly down the sidewalk. We waved to each other, she came in, walking directly to place her order. A few minutes later, she was at our table. We hugged. She sat down and we talked about ourselves. Lindsey told us she was from Tasmania originally.

"I escaped from there about 15 years ago."

"Why do you say escaped?" said Kat.

"Well, because its ultra conservative, you know, in the Bible Belt. When I came out as a lesbian, my mother suggested I leave Tasmania straight away, so no one would find out. I did, moved to Sydney. My ex-boyfriend found out where I lived and came over to knock the hell out of me." "Oh my god," I said shocked.

"Jesus," responded Kat.

"It's still a crime in Tasmania to be a lesbian," said Lindsey.

While Kat and I were enjoying a comfortable existence together as two women traveling, I looked at Lindsey and said, "I'm so sorry that you've had to go through all this, Lindsey." She looked at Kat and I and smiled.

"No drama, it's ok, just letting you know why I'm so far from home."

"Now you sheilas tell me about yourselves."

I looked at Kat and smiled. Kat hesitated.

"Well," she said, "we met through a friend. Then we started traveling together and now we're lovers but when we leave here, we'll be friends again." I didn't know our current relationship was effecting her so.

"I'm not sure I understand," said Lindsey.

"What she means is that we were good friends before this trip and somehow we became very close, so we feel like a couple, but when we get back home, Kat will go back to Massachusetts and I will go back to California, and those two places are not close together. They're as far apart as Sydney and Perth."

"Oh."

"Why don't one of you move in with the other?"

"Because we both have jobs that we've worked hard to get," said Kat "and we'd like to keep them."

"How long are you staying in Perth?"

"Another day or two."

"Have you been here for a while?"

"About a week."

"That's not a very long vacation for such a long trip from America," said Lindsey.

Kat leaned forward in her chair and said, "Well, actually, Lindsey, we've been in Australia for almost a month. We started in Sydney and drove from there to here through Canberra, Adelaide, Melbourne, and Kalgoorlie."

"Crikey, you sheilas are mental." We laughed. "What made you want to drive across our big country?"

"Jan's always been in love with your country."

"That's right," I chimed in. The three of us sat together talking for several hours. By the time we decided to leave and go our own ways, it was well after 2 PM and the coffee house people were kicking us out.

"Would you like to join us for lunch tomorrow at our apartment? It will be our last day and we'll cook some tucker for you?"

Lindsey smiled and said, "Sure." We drove back to the apartment, and as soon as we arrived, slammed the door shut and reenacted the "sinking ship," "clothes on fire" thing.

Lindsey arrived at about 12 noon. We each fixed a plate of food, grabbed a drink and hiked out to the umbrella tables by the pool. After lunch, we chit chatted about each other in intimate detail. I noticed that whenever Lindsey spoke to Kat, she leaned forward in her chair. She was quite taken with Kat.

"So, Lindsey, tell me what you do for a living," Said Kat.

"I'm an arborist."

"An arborist?" repeated Kat.

"Yeah," said Lindsey.

"Where is it you work?"

"At Kings Park."

"We know that park," I said. "It's beautiful. We've been there a couple of times. How long have you been working there, taking care of the park's trees?"

"Almost five years."

"Do you like what you do?"

"Yeah. What do you sheilas do?"

"I'm a park ranger, and Jan works in pediatric cardiology." We talked until the late afternoon. "How did you get here, Lindsey?"

"I took the rail and bus."

"Why don't we give you a lift back home?"

"Would you mind taking Lindsey yourself?" I said. "I want to start packing." I said goodbye to Lindsey, then she and Kat headed out.

By the time Kat returned from taking Lindsey home, it was almost 9:00. It was very clear that they had been intimate. I felt very hurt. I thought to myself, does she have to have sex with every woman that she meets? In the morning, Kat was up and packing the car. We were both very quiet.

When she finally spoke, she said. "She's not as exciting as you are!"

"Oh please, who couldn't see that coming? You act like a man sometimes, Kat, the way you are so cavalier about sex."

"You said yourself, Jan, that you and Kate get together only infrequently. You can't tell me that both of you don't seek other woman in the interim."

"Of course, we do, but we pick and choose, we don't do every woman we meet."

When the car was packed, we turned in the keys, finished the last pack of bagels, and hit the road to drive back across the continent. Kat and I spent the better part of the week trying to figure a route back across the country so that we wouldn't end up on some one-lane dirt road in the middle of the dessert with no idea of where to find the next petrol station. We first retraced our route from Perth to Norseman, and when we were near Port Augusta, we could start going north. Along this route, we would be passing the Nullarbor Plain again at the edge of the Great Victoria Dessert. We'd be a few days doing this drive, even if we pulled some all-nighters. Kat, however, refused to drive all day and all night, fearing that the exhaustion would get us in trouble. I reluctantly agreed.

On our second day of travel, we talked about what happened in Perth with Lindsey. Kat admitted that sex with Lindsey was very nonplus, but having it with you makes me feel, well, almost domestic and monogamous, kind of protective even, and while I went through the moves with Lindsey, it wasn't the same as it is with you. I'm not in a relationship with you, however, if we lived closer, I would be willing to try that.

"I can say with certainty that will never happen, Kat. I don't think you could ever leave your parties behind. Good grief, how long have you been having birthday parties at the hotels?"

"I started that when I met Kate." I was shocked.

"You're lying!" I yelled.

"I'm not, it's the truth. I was so taken with her, and it was clear that she wouldn't be exclusive with me. She was at an age where she was having a good time."

"When was that?" I said, not believing her.

"When she was near graduating from Brown. My cousin went to Brown and he brought Kate home a couple of times. It was very clear that she was not into him, but she hinted to me that she wanted to be with women, more than one. The only way I could have her was with other women, so I arranged it. From that time on, she came to most of my parties."

"She never told me about those parties," I said.

"Why would she?"

"Because I was her best friend. If she came to most of your parties, she was seeing you a lot more than she was seeing me." I was furious, hurt by Kate and Kat. I felt betrayed. I didn't know whether I loved them for trying, even in the least, to protect me from all of it or whether I hated them both for being so conniving. I decided for the next few hours, anyway, I was going to hate them both.

"Kat, I know that neither one of you was obligated to think of me when you were trying to do every woman in a 20-mile radius. But I'm really angry at both of you right now and I would prefer to have a little cry, get it out of my system, and think about how I'm going to handle all the shit I just heard. So, if you don't mind, I won't really feel like talking for a while."

Kat was at the wheel and she looked very serious. She nodded her head to let me know she understood. My eyes teared up. I had my little cry but knew just exactly what she meant, I'd felt differently about Kat as well.

"You're going to laugh," Kat said, "but at this moment, my brain zagged right into (and she sang a few bars) I've grown accustomed to your face!"

I sat stoned face trying to look like I was pissed off, but it was no use. I started giggling while she hummed another bar. I laughed even harder and Kat, who was trying hard to keep it together, let go and gave into a huge snort then laughed. The two of us continued to laugh until Kat finally had to pull over to deal with the hysterics. It took a few minutes before composure was regained. Kat reached over and hugged me. We drove for the next couple of hours in complete silence.

At Port Augusta, we began going north, passing three lakes, leaving the Simpson Dessert, and driving to Birdsville at the edge of the Great Artesian Basin. At Birdsville, we drove east/north/east toward Longreach and east again into Mackay and the Great Barrier Reef. It took nearly a week to go north back across the country. From here on out, traveling would be uncomplicated. Even though we had a few more stops, we would be on the same coastal route, south, until we reached Sydney.

On arriving in Mackay, we took a ride to the coast.

"Did you ever doubt that you would get here, Jan?"

"Never!" We got a hotel room and unpacked the car, then went into town to figure out how we were going to get out to the reef.

Whitsunday air transport advertised trips to the reef, so did about four other airplane companies. We went with "Whitsunday." Craig the pilot would take us out there at 9 AM tomorrow morning. Wear a bather (swim suit), but bring clothes for over the suit, preferably a top with long sleeves. Load up on sunblock and wear a hat. Wear runners (sneakers) that can protect your feet from the razor-sharp coral, and by all means, bring a camera. When we showed at the dock, there were several planes loading and taking off. Kat and I climbed in, she in front and me in the back. We each had a backpack with water, a small first aid kit, snacks, towel, binoculars, flippers, snorkel, and mask and a camera.

We wore our clothes over our swim suits and had our hats on. When we landed, it was right next to the reef. We got out of the plane and stepped out onto the reef. We could see where the shallow reef water was and where there was a significant drop off that looked to be hundreds of feet deep. You could actually see large sharks swimming in the deep water, but where the reef was, it was too shallow for them to swim.

Craig stepped out on the reef and said, "Don't take anything from the reef. It's our national treasure and we want to preserve it. Walk on the reef as little as possible, and stay out of the deep water unless you want to be brunch for the great White."

We took off our hats, shorts, and shirts, put on our flippers, mask and snorkel and headed into the water. Craig held up his watch arm and shouted, "You have two hours."

We trolled around the reef, disbelieving what we were seeing. The life was abundant, the colors were fantastic. Looking at the water, one would never expect that so much life lay below it! We saw a ginormous grouper, biggest one I ever saw, and in the Great Lakes, they can get pretty big! We saw Clown fish, Sun fish, Groupers, Eels, Lion fish, a huge turtle swimming out to sea. There were Baramundi, Barracuda, and Cleaner fish. At one point, we spotted a giant clam resting open in the sun. The meat in it was iridescent purple, blue, green. The colors were just so brilliant. I looked at it and wondered if I could just touch the edge of this beautiful creature and then thought better of it. Kat stood back and watched as I took a small piece of shell and lobbed it in the clam. To my surprise, that clam slammed its top shell so quickly, the force of the water pushed me back. Both of us shot to the surface.

"Oh my god," said Kat, "are you ok?"

"I'm fine."

"What made you do that?"

"I don't know, just curious."

"Oh, ok, next time you get curious to try to kill yourself, give me a warning, and I'll get out of your way!"

"Sorry, I didn't mean to scare you," I said. Kat looked at me like she wanted to hurt me.

We snorkeled for every minute of the two hours. When we got back to the plane, Craig was holding a pregnant reef shark. Reef sharks are very small compared to their cousins swimming in the deep water.

We flew back to Mackay and I asked Craig about going out again tomorrow.

"I don't have any clients that have booked the plane yet. We'll go to a different spot than yesterday."

"That's ok, we just want to see more," I said.

"Yes, it's fascinating," said Kat.

"Ok, be here at 9 AM." We were, and it was just as exciting as the day before. Since there wasn't much else to do in Mackay, we decided to head south on the third day. Brisbane was 803 km. or 498 mi. It would take us about 11 hours to get there.

Kat drove when we approached Brisbane.

"I know next to nothing about this city," I said.

"It looks pretty sizable," said Kat.

"Let me see what I can find," I said, perusing the book I'd purchased this trip and found a few things. "It's the Capitol of Queensland. It's known as the Sunshine State. It has a population of over a million and is the third largest city in Australia. Brisbane is the cultural epicenter for Australia. It started as a place where a penal colony was set up."

"I don't know if I'm just tired, but this is not catching my interest."

"Yes, let me tell you about the things to do. We plan on checking out Story Bridge."

"Right," said Kat. "I hear you can climb the bridge."

"That's what I hear. The other thing I am interested in," I said "are the paintings of the Stars at the Queens. There is the Gallery of Modern Art. There is also Lone Pine Kangaroo Sanctuary. That should be fun."

We spent three days in Brisbane and the Gold Coast, being entertained by the Kangaroo Sanctuary and the Gallery of Modern Art. Kat was anxious to see the paintings that the Stars did. But she was even more anxious to hit the Gold Coast, which was an hour south of Brisbane.

"I can't wait to get on a board!" After we rented a catamaran, which was absolutely exhilarating! Kat wanted to rent a couple of wind surf boards.

Despite our fun, we needed to get back on the road. It was 749 km or 466 mi. and ten hours of driving to Sydney. These long days of driving were really starting to get to us. However, we had to return the rental and we had a trip of rest planned to New Zealand. On the eighth of December, Kat and I pulled into Sydney late at night. We drove to the Radisson in downtown and checked in for the night. We brought our bags up with us, asked for a wake-up call at 9 AM, peeled off our clothes, and fell into bed.

Nine o'clock came around way too quickly. I felt like I could sleep the day away. I did not want to be the first in the shower because it meant I could sleep 15 more minutes.

"Get up," I said to Kat. "Get up and get in the shower, I'll order some breakfast, what do you want?"

"You," she said.

"Well, I'm not up for grabs this morning, we need to get out or they'll charge us for another day."

"That's ok, isn't it?" "No, it's not. Come on, get in the shower."

"Ok, you're such a nudge. I'll have a Danish and some coffee."

I picked up the phone and ordered, then crawled back under the covers. A knock on the door woke me. I pulled on my bathrobe and answered the door and took our meal. Kat came bounding out of the bathroom like a golden retriever.

"Your turn, flower!"

I grabbed a bite of the toast and a sip of the tea and went into the shower.

We were downstairs by ten o'clock. We checked out and drove to the car rental place. It was in the airport complex. How different everything felt. Now we were both used to left side driving. We pulled in a space and went in.

"G'day." The gal at the counter was smiling and appeared to like her job.

"Good morning," I said. She smiled again and you could see "tourist" go through her brain.

"Can I help you?" I was thinking she's was really charming.

Kat whispered in my ear, "She's hot!"

I gave Kat a dirty look and then responded with, "I'd like to turn in the rental I have."

"Do you have your paper work?" she asked.

"Yes." And I handed it over.

"Do you have the number of kilometers that you put on the car?"

"Yes," and I couldn't wait to see her reaction.

"13,738.97 km!"

"Pardon me."

"13,738.97km." She was writing and looked up from her paper.

"1,300 km?"

"No, it's 13,738.97 km or 8,532 miles." She wasn't smiling anymore.

"1,300 km?"

"No, ma'm, 13,738.97 km. We had it tuned up in Perth."

She finally responded again, "1,300?"

"No, 13,738.97 km."

"I see," she said.

She made a very quiet call to her boss, no doubt, and we waited. A gentleman in a white shirt and tie approached the counter. She showed him the paper and he looked it over.

"G'day. Ma'm, we're just trying to understand how many km. you put on the car."

I was starting to be annoyed, it wasn't funny anymore.

"13,738.97 km."

He excused himself and went to the car and looked at the odometer. He wrote the kilometers down. He came back to the counter and looked at the sheet.

Kat finally spoke and said, "Is there a problem?"

"It's just a little unusual to see this many km. on a rental."

"Look, mate, we drove from Sydney to Perth and back across the deserts to the Barrier Reef and back down to Sydney. We had unlimited mileage and unlimited locales with no restrictions to state lines. So, this may be unusual for you, but there it is in black and white, mate, and there is our contract behind it. We've got stuff to do today in your lovely city and we would very much appreciate it if you could wrap this up."

We paid up, and when he handed us our receipts, he said, "If you have any future rental needs, you might check with our neighbors" and he pointed to the rental place across the way.

"Don't worry, Jack," I said, "We have no plans of renting from you again."

We walked out and waited for the bus to take us to the Bondi Beach.

After the bus dropped us at Bondi, Kat went for some lunch and I called Mark and Julie. We found a place to change into our suits and then we threw our towels in the sand, put our heavy bags down, groaned, and laid down on the warm sand. It was summer here now. The kids were out of school for a couple of months and Christmas and the New Year were right around the corner! Isn't it weird to hear Christmas songs when the weather is like this?" said Kat.

"I dunno, I could get used to it."

"Jan, are you considering moving here?"

"I think about it now and again."

"You think we'll see Philippa and Nora and Charlene and Ruthie?" I asked. "They sounded like they were really hoping to make it to the U.S. someday. What about Lindsey?" Kat looked a bit sheepish.

"I don't know about her." Kat put her head on her hands and exhaled loudly.

We stayed for two days with Julie and Mark before going to New Zealand. On December 11th, we left for the North Island of New Zealand, we had rented a cabin on Rotorua Lake in the town of Rotorua. It was a little like a mountain cabin, small and quaint. In the mornings, they delivered milk with cream on top in glass bottles, some scones, and a newspaper. The second day we were there, we went out in kayaks and did some fishing. I caught a 15" trout. The cut off length was 12". We saved some milk and scones and put a trout dinner together. It was delicious! Thankfully I could still remember how to clean a fish. We went swimming, read books, and went to a local Maori ceremony. The owner was very attentive and seemed to genuinely like us. She was a retired school teacher. Life couldn't get any better, unless Kate walked in the door! Kat was playful as always and we talked a lot and worked a lot of stuff out. We decided, or rather I decided, that I wouldn't let Kat's indiscretion affect my relationship with her or the rest of the trip. I did have a good time with her.

In my head, I hoped that I would be with Kate one day, I half expected I would when she got things out of her system. I knew Kat would always be a good friend to me and I to her. But I really didn't understand her pathology around sex with multiple women. I thought it was about Kate, but when I asked Kat if she would still have the parties if Kate didn't go, she said she would!

We'd been through "some shit" on this trip.

"You know, Kat. I'm going to make a reverse drive that my father made in 1958 down the Alcan Highway from Alaska to the lower 48."

"When are you doing that?"

"I'm not sure. I just know I'm doing it."

"Well, keep me posted on that one."

I grabbed my wallet and Kat said, "Where are you going?"

"I keep pictures in my wallet."

"That's a good idea."

"Can I look at them with you?"

"Sure."

The first one I pulled out was of Kate and me when we were kids, arms around each other. Then came Kate, Charlie, and me.

"Who's the other guy with you?"

"Charlie's friend, Bernie."

Then I pulled a picture of Kate when she graduated from Brown. The next one I had was of Kat, Kate, and Terry, then Robert Hart and his five daughters.

"One thing is very apparent, Jam."

"Yeah, I know. Well that's it for the pictures." Kat looked over at me with raised eyebrows. "What now?" she said. I leaned over and kissed her.

We connected with Julie and Mark again when we returned to Sydney. They asked that we come and stay with them until we took off for the states. They took us to a few places in Sydney that we would not have otherwise gone to. One evening, Julie, Mark, David, Kat and I went to dinner at a wonderful restaurant that revolved so that every hour, we would have seen the entire city of Sydney. We had five tickets at the Sydney Opera House to see the Nutcracker after dinner. Our last day in Sydney, the five of us would take a hike on the Sydney Harbor Bridge. It was pretty spectacular but not for the faint of heart! We had safety harnesses on, but the height still scared me.

The morning of our departure, we woke to the birds screeching good morning. Julie, Mark, and David took us to the airport. It was difficult to say goodbye. They were so far away. David picked up on my mood and remarked that it was just a 16-hour flight. Plan it for a long weekend. We laughed, hugged, and boarded for the trip home.

"You don't look as upset as I thought you would be," said Kat.

"I think perhaps I'll be back, I want to see the reef again and we never did make it to Ayer's Rock."

"What do you think, Kat."

"I'm up for a trip back. Left sided driving is a piece of cake."

"Wait till you get home and try to drive Yankee style again!"

Until 1997, being gay in Tasmania was against the law and you could be put in jail.

Until 1974, being gay in the U.S. was considered a mental illness. In 1974, it was taken out of the Psychology Manuel as such.

— ◆ —

Kookaburra

Kookaburra sits on the old gum tree,
Merry merry king of the bush is he.
Laugh, Kookaburra, laugh, Kookaburra,
Gay your life must be!
Kookaburra sits in the old gum tree
Eating all the gumdrops he can see
Stop, Kookaburra, Stop, Kookaburra
Leave some there for me.
Kookaburra sits in the old gum tree,
Counting all the monkeys he can see
Stop, Kookaburra, Stop, Kookaburra,
That's no monkey, that's me.

— ◆ —

Waltzing Matilda

Once a Jolly swagman camped by a billabong
Under the shade of a Coolibah tree,
He sang as he watched and waited 'til his billy boiled
You'll come a-Waltzing Matilda, with me
Waltzing Matilda, Waltzing Matilda
You'll come a-Waltzing Matilda, with me
He sang as he watched and waited 'til his billy boiled,
 you'll come a-Waltzing Matilda, with me
Down came a jumbuck to drink at the billabong,
Up jumped the swagman and grabbed him with glee,
 he sang as he shoved that jumbuck in his tucker bag,
 you'll come a-Waltzing Matilda, with me

Waltzing Matilda, Waltzing Matilda
you'll come a-Waltzing Matilda, with me
he sang as he shoved that jumbuck in his tucker bag,
You'll come a-Waltzing Matilda, with me
Up rode the squatter, mounted on his thoroughbred,
Up rode the troopers, one, two, three,
With the Jolly jumbuck you've got in your tucker bag?
You'll come a-Waltzing Matilda, with me.
Waltzing Matilda, Waltzing Matilda
You'll come a-Waltzing Matilda, with me
With the Jolly jumbuck you've got in your tucker bag?
You'll come a-Waltzing Matilda, you scoundrel with me.
Up jumped the swagman and sprang into the billabong,
You'll never catch me alive, said he,
And his ghost may be heard as you pass by that billabong,
you'll come a-Waltzing Matilda, with me.
Waltzing Matilda, Waltzing Matilda
You'll come a-Waltzing Matilda, with me
his ghost may be heard as you pass by that billabong,
You'll come a-Waltzing Matilda, with me.
Oh, you'll come a-Waltzing Matilda, with me

Chapter Eleven

Goodby to All That

I don't think I've ever written about my mother, but at the time of her death on Wednesday, September 3rd, 2014, it was a pretty ordinary day, hump day to those still working. I was 58, my baby sister was 52, the sister between us, 53, my brother next to me, 62, and my oldest brother was 65. My mother was 90-years-old, an age she thought she would never see.

As a kid, I used to lay in my room and calculate all of our ages. If I was 30, then Jack would be 37, Joe, 34, Joan, 25 and Julia, 24. I even went up to 50 for me, and for some reason, that was as high as I would go, I felt that was old!

When growing up, I looked at my mother with my kid eyes. She was size 16, not fat, but robust, with an average height of 5'6". She seemed like a pretty powerful woman. At 90, she was barely 5' and 100 lbs. I think of all the things that shocked me about my mother getting old, it was how little and frail she would become!

I was constantly looking for clothes to fit her, either in the 0 section of Chico's or in the children's section of Goodwill. I never told her about the kid's section of Goodwill because it just didn't seem dignified. Her favorite thing that I found at Goodwill was a child's Norwegian's sweater, navy blue with metal clasps.

"Where ever did you find it?" she wanted to know. I'd smile kind of sly-like and say in a Yiddish accent.

"I 'ave my haunts you no!"

By the time I was a teenager, my mother and I were constantly butting heads. I felt she was impossible to get along with. My father always testified to that. They fought frequently. And for many years, after a fight, my mother could be found in the bedroom crying and my father in the darkened living room, the only light coming from his cigarette. I would walk by and see him there and would sit in his chair next to him.

He would put his arm around me and whisper, "I don't know what to do to make your mother happy."

By the time I was 13, I didn't stop when I walked through the dark living room anymore. My dad sat by himself with the single light of his cigarette.

In high school, I had a renewed surge trying to form some bond with my mother. But the outcome was always the same. She was controlling, demanding, and difficult. All I could think of was getting out of there, I just didn't want to hear her scream and holler and say really awful things to everyone when she was mad as she did with great regularity. In May of 1975, I packed one large backpack, got my passport, emptied my bank account, and took off for Europe to see some friends.

My parting words to my sister were, "Don't ever call me to come take care of her. I will send money, help you negotiate her medical stuff, send birthday, anniversary, and Christmas cards, but don't ask for me to take care of her. I won't do it."

When my parents retired and every child had left home, I tried talking to my oldest brother about my parents getting old and what the care for them would look like. But each time I gave it over and felt like he was an idiot. He felt like I was a worry wort. Even when my father was in his early 80's, Jack called me to ask if I wanted to chip in for my dad's birthday and buy him a bike. "What kind of bike? Like a three-wheel bike?"

"No, that's for an old person, an English-Racer."

"Jack, he is an old person, he is 81! And they live on a dirt road with a lot of stones. Don't you think that is dangerous?"

"No."

"I do, I'll get him something else."

"So, you don't want to go in with everyone?"

"No."

Conversation with my brother Joe didn't go much better, mainly because he was high all the time. And if the rest of the sibs were going in with Jack, then nobody was taking the time or energy to consider my parents old age.

When we were kids, my mother taught Sunday School, went to church, and dragged all of our asses to the same. But when my mother found out that her oldest daughter was a lesbian, she launched headlong into her bible thumping mode. My liking woman rather than men seemed to throw her into a kind of religious breakdown. She started reading the bible to everyone and went to bible study several days a week. She played only religious music in the house and went crazy if someone changed the radio station. She had a huge influence on my siblings, and by the time I was in my 30's, all my sibs stopped contact with me to stay in her good graces. My father and I maintained contact because I would call home on Sunday while my mother was out playing the organ for three different churches in their very small town. We would start our conversation the same way each time.

"Hi, Dad, you by yourself?"

"Yes, your mother is at church, she might as well set up a God damn cot down there!"

Eventually, my father and I came to an understanding that I would not call anymore because my mother gave him too much grief when I did, and I didn't want to make it harder for him.

My father had been diagnosed with heart disease and he had already had one heart attack. My parents made the decision to sell their house on the river and leave the frozen north country, so that they could be near their kids and a hospital. We recommended that my mom move them to a place that had a sizeable hospital, one with a competent cardiac unit.

I followed them as they made their way from their home to Syracuse, where my oldest brother lived, to Colorado, where my sister lived, to Northern California where my middle brother and baby sister lived. I was living in the same area as my middle brother but by then we hadn't spoken for years.

I had my parents on my mind constantly for months. I didn't really know exactly where they were or what was going on in their lives, but I had this dread that I needed to contact them soon. So, I started calling but got no response from my brothers and sisters. I surmised that they were in California. Maybe living with my brother. I googled them and found their names in Vallejo, CA. Vallejo? I knew no one in Vallejo except our friend Carly, who was assistant warden at San Quentin, who had a house there. We'd been to Vallejo many times for her memorable parties. But what were my parents doing in Vallejo? They had a telephone number listed beside their names, so I jotted it down and went out to run errands for the morning.

I couldn't stop thinking about them. I got home and couldn't put it off any longer. I sat down and dialed. It rang about four times and then I heard my mother's aged voice, "Hello?"

"Mom, this is Janet."

"Yes, I saw you on the caller ID."

She sounded very old – she was 83. We talked for several minutes and then I asked her about my father.

"He isn't like he was."

"What do you mean?"

"He fell on the concrete and hit his head." I was shocked. But I already knew what she would say. "He had severe trauma to his head." It felt like the floor just dropped from beneath me. It was a kind of horror I knew would have changed him. It felt like a spear penetrating my heart. She, of course, did not put him on the phone.

"Mom, I'd like to visit you and Dad."

We made arrangements to do so.

Over the next few months, my mother my Partner Jill and I began to form relationships with each other. Having a relationship with my mother seemed strange. I remembered her when I was very little and she would read books to me and appeared to be a normal mother, but when I was 12 or 13, things began to change and we grew to hate each other. It felt different now because we were both adults on equal footing; and though we would talk about when I was small, I never felt as though I was dealing with the same person because I wasn't.

My mother's name was Anna Virginia, but she went by her middle name, Virginia. Jill called her Anna (just to irk her, I think). My father knew me and remembered Jill (he met her once). He was indeed different in that he was very docile. My mother at 83 was his only care giver. A CNA came in to bathe him twice a week and he created a ruckus when that happened. Neither my brothers nor my sisters visited with any great consistency or not at all. My mother said he had some dementia, but after the fall, his dementia kicked into high gear. It was clear that quite a bit of damage was sustained when he fell, and yet, he still maintained his sense of humor and love of music.

During the next few months, my mother and I began to look for a facility for my father that was in Vallejo. When we finally found the right place, we set him up there and everything was as good as it could be. My mother visited him every day. All my brothers and sisters were called and told of his new digs. He and my mother were in good spirits. Even though they were living apart for the first time in their 60 years of marriage, things felt easier for Mom. She wasn't worrying about how she could or couldn't take care of him and the staff loved my father and took decent care of him. He reveled in the attention.

My father was changing though. Ever so slowly, he would smile or laugh, but he wasn't the one to do the teasing anymore. He would cry when he reminisced about special times with my mother, the loss of his brother or friends during the war. At the beginning and throughout his stay in the facility, he constantly tried to romance my mother.

"Virginia, I want to live like man and wife again. Turn on Lawrence Welk and come sit next to me!" He would grab my mother and plant a kiss on her cheek. "Stay with me tonight, Virginia." She would smile and hug him, "I can't stay, Jake, they won't let me stay."

"We'll hide you under the covers."

"Let's listen to Lawrence Welk, Jake." Every day would end this way and my mother, if she tired of it, she never let on. She just kept smiling.

Jill would come out to visit with me when she could, usually on the weekends. The first time she witnessed my father's romantic interludes, she said to me, as we were driving home. "You know, I just can't get past hearing your dad try and convince your mother to have sex while sitting in his diapers!"

During the days when I drove to Vallejo, I would take my parents to their favorite haunt, Arby's drive thru. They loved the sandwiches with "horsey sauce." This particular day, I had Jill's PT cruiser convertible and my folks were enjoying the spring-time sun, at least my mother was, my father seemed off that day. As we settled in to eat our sandwiches, I set my father up with his drink and food. I was several bites into my lunch and looked over to see my father gnawing on his sandwich. He hadn't bitten it at all.

"Dad, can you take a bite of your sandwich?" He tried to, but it was apparent he could not. I took it from him and gave him something to drink. As easily as that, his and our lives changed. He was in a new phase of life, that much closer to dying. I'd been in the medical field long enough to know that he when the food situation changed and he stopped eating that it wouldn't be a whole lot longer. He went through puree and being fed. When we visited him during this time, he was always in bed. He couldn't stand or walk anymore. By Thanksgiving ,he was rapidly declining.

My mother and I had many talks about my father. She would tell me stories of their travels and courtship. It was as if she wanted me to know everything about my father. By December, he wasn't talking anymore. My mother played Christmas carols on the piano in the facility's common room. I would put my dad in his wheelchair and take him out to listen. He really enjoyed that. A day or two before Christmas, my mother was playing *White Christmas*, my dad's favorite Christmas song. I got on my knees and put my arm around him and my head on his shoulder. My father's voice had punctuated my growing up. I could hear his beautiful tenor voice articulate a song in my head. It was hard to believe I would never hear him sing again. I began singing softly in his ear, and out of the corner of my eye, I could see him mouth the words to the song, though he had no voice. I tried hard not to cry, fearing he would stop, but could not hold back the tears. As my mother played, she glanced at my father and I and she began to cry but continued to play the song through to the end. It was the last song that he sang, if only to himself.

Hospice got involved. Jill and I planned to spend New Year's Eve at a friend's in Sacramento. My mother was staying with my brother Joe. At 4 PM on New Year's Eve, hospice called to say that my father's breathing was slowing. They felt that he would pass tonight or tomorrow. We'd been singing and having a good time. Jill and I slowly got our stuff together. Jill's sister Jean came over, hugged and kissed me. I was crying while trying to pull on my boots. They had lost their mother six months before.

Jean sat down next to me and said, "Tell him everything you want him to know, Janet. Talk to him, tell him everything." I nodded to her and we left. I called my sister and brother in the Bay Area and we began our drive back to Vallejo.

On the road to Vallejo, the sky was fog with one fine thin line of sunset at the horizon. As we drove, the line of fog got smaller and the sunset colors filled in wider and wider until the sky was the most brilliant orange, pink, yellow, and red that I had ever seen.

I thought about my parents and renewing my relationship with both of them. It was with my father's need for care and placement in a facility and his gradual decline that my mother and I drew closer and closer together. In the beginning of our relationship, as two adults, we tackled issues from my childhood and gradually worked into my being a lesbian. She was surprisingly open and accepting now. I didn't know what happened, but it didn't much matter. We bonded as mother and daughter. Taking care of my father brought us together as mother and daughter in a labor of love.

When we arrived, my sister Julia, who had been waiting outside for us, practically threw herself crying into my arms. She was the baby in the family and had stayed with my parents the longest of any of us. She and my dad were as close as I was to my father. Once inside, my brother Joe, who hadn't bothered to talk to me in years, greeted me by grabbing me and hugging for the longest time. My mother looked sad and heart broken. She was losing the love of her life of 60 years. She was bereft. I concentrated on her, stood by her as she took my father's hand, and kissed it.

"Mom, have you had anything to eat?" She shook her head and my brother announced that he and his wife, Julia, and Mom were going to dinner. Did we want to join them? Jill and I stayed behind.

We talked to the staff and they had a bedroom we could use if one of us needed to lay down. Julia, Jill and I agreed to stay with Mom for as long as it would take. I'd prepared my sister and mother for hospice's practice of giving morphine about a week before. I explained it to them again. They had dropped off vials for us to give to him. After my brother and sister-in-law left, a nurse went over what to administer. I did the first hour with some given every hour. My father was restless and his breathing was becoming labored. We all took turns sitting with him. Julia and I laid our heads next to him and talked to him. When it was my mother's turn, she laid next to him and was silent.

"What should I say, Janet?"

"Tell him how much you love him, Mom. Talk about your life together. Tell him everything." They say that the hearing is the last to go when you're dying. I believe that to be true. It felt good to me that we could send my father off with the love we felt for him. On January 1st, 2008, at 1:04 AM, my father's spirit left this world.

Jill left for home about 2 AM. My sister, mother and I went back to Mom's apartment. We slept about two hours and my mother came tip toeing into the living room where Julia and I were sleeping.

"Janet, get up, let's get some breakfast. Julia is asleep."

"So was I."

She just smiled; I got up, put on my boots and jacket, and we left to eat. As my mother drove down El Camino, it was cold at 7 AM.

"Mom, it just doesn't feel real."

"I know. It doesn't feel as though I've lost the only man I've loved for 60 years." We went into a small breakfast place and it was humming with people. I looked around and thought how strange it was to have just lost my father and the world was still turning, people still talking and laughing.

"I always thought I would go first," my mother smiled in a sad sort of way. I choked back a few tears and my mother did the same. It was New Year's Day, Jill's and my anniversary.

After my father's death, my mother felt isolated and lonely. She was 35 miles away from Jill and I on the peninsula. When Dad passed, his military retirement ceased and it dropped Mom's income substantially. Reality was that she could no longer afford to live where she was unless she had money coming in.

"There are insurance policies, Janet, that I can collect and one very large one."

I remember my father saying that when he died that "your mother will be set for life," of course implying that there was indeed a large policy to collect on. The following day, Jill and I went out to Vallejo to help. We knew nothing about her finances, but she was due to receive $1,500 from one policy and $1,000 from another, and those would not sustain her when her rent alone was $2,300. About mid-afternoon, we had still only found the smaller policies. My mother brought out a couple more boxes and then left the room for several minutes. Jill and I discovered a policy in one of the boxes for nearly a million dollars, but the look on her face indicated that something was wrong. My mother returned and we told her what we found. We suggested that we take it back home and look at the paper work. It was getting late and we had two dogs to feed.

I learned through Julia that my brothers knew about the policy and were convinced I renewed my relationship with my parents, so I could get the money from the policy. It was ridiculous. Why would they think that way unless they entertained those thoughts?

On closer examination, it was very clear that the policy had lapsed. The premiums had not been paid in a couple of years and there was no way to collect on the policy, and it in fact, would have paid nearly a million dollars! We talked about what to do. She had $35,000 to her name and my brother Joe was holding that for her. We expected that she would live a while, she was pretty healthy, and $35,000 was not going to help much. We decided to try and convince her to move to the peninsula and get a small apartment there, where she could be close to us and she wouldn't have to pay such a large amount every month to be at the assisted care place. We laid our suggestions out for her to see if she was agreeable. She was, and the week following, I found an apartment in a neat little complex in South San Francisco. She would be five minutes away from Jill at work and 17 minutes from our house. But best of all, she would be right next door to the Senior Center!

We got her packed up, arranged the movers, and transferred her money to Jill's Credit Union, where Jill worked as an Executive Vice President. She stayed with us for a couple of days until the movers brought her belongings.

My mother's spirits seem to be on the upswing. Jill and I fixed up my mother's apartment with curtains and a new bed spread and flowers on her porch. My mother was in her element, still missing my dad, but enjoying life. She joined the Senior Center, found a knitting and crocheting group there, and made a few friends. She Joined the Baptist Church just down the street from her. She learned the drive from her place to ours. When she went to her new Credit Union, Jill took time to visit with her. My mother continued our talks about my father and ourselves. My sister Julia came from the city and joined us for outings.

Mom even took to flirting a bit, which really surprised me, because in her former life, it wasn't a behavior she even thought about. When I took her to the grocery store on one occasion, she was in a motorized scooter and a gentleman of a similar age stood behind her. I was at the end of the counter waiting to get the groceries and throw them in a bag. When I looked up this man, who was obviously admiring her hair, which was a beautiful white color, picked up a curl and held it gingerly in his fingers. I immediately jumped to and wanted to know what the hell he was doing! My mother turned around and smiled.

"You have the prettiest hair." What did he think he was doing? Mom now tried to run her card through the machine to pay, but it wasn't registering. The gentleman behind took her card and ran it through for her.

I took her card from him and heard myself say, "I'll do that for her, I'm her daughter."

As we finished and started out of the store, my mother stopped me, smiled, and said, "Janet, it's ok. He was harmless."

"He was proprietary."

She laughed and said, "He was harmless."

One of the first Thanksgivings my mother spent with Jill and I after she moved to the peninsula, was a big gathering. We had some old friends from Rome, a total of 11 people. During the meal, our friend asked my mom if there were any men at the Senior Center that interested her.

"Well, maybe one," was her response.

My sister Julia looked at her, shocked, "Mom? Really? How could you?"

"Julia, are you that much of a prude?"

We were all chuckling about Mom teasing her, but Mom brought the house down when she very calmly remarked, "Julia, there might be snow on the roof, but there is a fire in the chimney!"

We all roared with laughter.

When my nephew Ben came to visit from Wisconsin, he would join us. He slept on his grandmother's floor and the four of us went site seeing in the Bay Area. Ben, even in his late 20's, still solicited advise from his grandmother.

In time, I began to notice that the route to our house and back home was suddenly different for her. She couldn't remember where to turn and she would forget other things, especially groceries. I found the book *The 36 Hour Day*, by Nancy L. Mace, a book about people getting dementia and how to care for them, what signs to look for. If my mother had it, she was hiding it very well. I pulled out some old photo albums and found a picture of her father at about age 30. The next day, I took the photo with me to my mom's.

I handed it to her and said, "I think you should have this, Mom."

She screwed up her face, letting me know without a doubt that she didn't know who she was looking at.

"Who is this, Janet?" My heart sank.

"It's your father, Mom."

"Oh, right, how silly of me."

After, I told Jill what I had discovered. I also told my baby sister and Ben.

The very next day, Julia and I were sitting with Mom in her apartment and Julia, without any warning, blurted out, "Mom, Janet thinks you're demented."

I looked at her in utter disgust. I couldn't imagine why she would do that. I wanted to kick her. "Mom, I've noticed that you're forgetting a lot of things lately."

My mother shook her head yes and her eyes filled with tears.

I went over and hugged her and said, "It's alright, I've scheduled an evaluation at the Over Sixty Clinic in Berkeley for you. We'll see what you're dealing with then, ok? Let's just wait and see what they have to say."

The evaluation concluded that she was in the early stages of Alzheimer's. I talked with her about drugs and she didn't want to take any. We would revisit that topic at least once more.

In the meantime, my brothers and one sister back east were not to be found. They weren't visiting and rarely called. This started after my father's death, but it was solidly in place now. Jill, Mom, Ben, Julia and I celebrated the holidays together. Eventually, my mother announced that she wanted to stop driving. I was surprised that she voluntarily gave up her driving, but had she not, I would have brought it up to her. She was gunning it between stop lights and signs and then hitting the brakes hard. It was only a matter of time before something happened. So, whenever she wanted to come over, I would pick her up and take her home.

When Jill's dad, Henry, needed to stop driving, he refused and his doctor wouldn't give us a note when we asked. He didn't want to be involved in what he felt was a family dispute. Jill and Jean tried everything, taking the keys, pulling off hoses, disconnecting wires. When nothing worked, his daughters wrote the doctor telling him they would hold him responsible if their father got into an accident and hurt someone or himself. The doctor wrote a letter to the DMV, and they finally got Henry off the road. So, my mother's voluntarily handing the keys over seemed like a cake walk compared to Henry.

My mother was constantly surprising me about conversation on certain topics, things that we never talked about before. They were little things that she seemed to pick out of the air. She asked me how I liked school.

"What school?"

"All of it."

"I've been to a lot of schools, Mom, you mean in Rome?"

"Yes, Laurel Street School, where you, Jack, and Joe all went together, and Rome Free Academy, where we all went in different decades? And what was your college like or nursing school?" I was confused. But then I realized that we never really talked about any of that. So, I told her.

Then she wanted to know how I fell in love with Jill and did I fall in love with her before Mike and I were divorced or after and did I divorce Mike because I liked Jill?

She also wanted to know what transpired with Mike and Julia (Mike was my ex-husband, also known as Shithead), an alcoholic who aspired to screw every woman he could. In fact, when I announced to friends and family that I was divorcing him, friends and family alike proclaimed that he had hit on them. Julia said relatively little about her relationship with him except that he had paid for her to move to Hawaii.

She was also curious about my medical situation, especially my back and the Parkinson's. How did falling out of the tree at nine have anything to do with my back now. We talked about my sibs and hers. My sister-in-law, Joe's wife, and Joe had embezzled hundreds of thousands of dollars from his wife's employer and had toured the world. My mother was loath to try and understand it.

She kept trying to insert disclaimers in the story, like, "Well, it was his wife who really did the embezzling."

"Yes, Mom, but if my brother is helping to spend the money, then he is part and parcel of the crime."

"How would he know where the money came from Janet?"

"Mom, if Jill came home one day with nearly a million dollars and we suddenly booked a trip around the world, the first thing I would say to her after 'holy shit' would be where did you come into so much money, love?"

"Right!"

In 1955, my mother was very pregnant with a sister who was to be named Virginia Anne. They had just arrived in Alaska. It was one of my father's last places to be transferred to for the Air Force. They sent him out to a job site on the Aleutian Islands off Alaska while my mother stayed behind and delivered within a week of arriving. The military, in all its screw-ups, pulled a big one and forgot to tell my father that his wife had delivered. They also forgot to mention that it was a baby girl and only lived two hours because she was born with undeveloped lungs; they had holes in them and it was not a diagnosis conducive with life in 1955.

I looked at my mother. It was the day Virginia Anne was born and died. My mother never talked about her, unlike my father whose pain over losing a child was palpable, even after some 50 years. I was born 11 months later, and my father joyfully sent off a message to the family in New York State. If she had lived, it would have changed the family. For one thing, we all wouldn't have been 'J' names and she would have been one year closer to Joe.

One morning, I was driving my mother back from a doctor's appointment. I was thinking about Julia on the drive over to Mom's. She had been a real pain all week and I was trying to find a way to deal with her.

It was March 9th, Virginia Anne's birthday.

"Mom, do you know what day it is today?"

"It's your sister Virginia Anne's birthday."

"Do you ever think about the dynamics of how the family would have changed if she had lived?" "Yes."

There was silence for a moment, then I said, "There might not have been a Julia." And I smiled a little.

My mother smiled at me and said, "There might not have been a Janet." We both chuckled.

In time, Julia became more difficult to deal with. She had a tentative hold on reality. She would have flare-ups of anger, that scared all of us. Julia eventually decided rather than visit Mom, she would just move in and save all that bus fare. She shopped for Mom, and when she picked up or ordered groceries for Mom, she ordered some for herself as well. She and Julia went to dinner or lunch and Mom paid for, both of them, all the time. When she borrowed her car, Mom paid for up-keep, any maintenance, tires, and gas. Anything Julia spent on anything was now from Mom.

Just after Christmas, Julia decided she wanted to get a job at See's Candy Factory, then she could have all the candy she could possibly want. She lined up an interview and borrowed Mom's car to get herself there. However, when she pulled out of the car lot, she ran into a car on the far side of the street and that car in turn hit another. Julia, with her questionable ethics, asked our mother if she would take the fall for the accident. My mother declined, and so Julia called my mother's car insurance company and added her name to the policy. When my mother told me about the accident, all the information about Julia moving in and spending money came to light.

Mom wanted Julia to leave and go back to her own apartment. My sister was severely mentally ill and had been there long enough to make my mother feel imprisoned in her own home. Julia was extremely paranoid and locked everything, including her suitcase and backpack. She would put tape on the doors at night to see if someone was coming in. She put an extra lock on my mother's front door. Julia was adamant that the woman above my mom was speaking to her through the bathroom light fixture.

We took control of Mom's checkbook and Jill reviewed and balanced it while we made plans to get Julia some help and tell her she would have to leave. Jill examined Mom's money situation and found that Julia had coerced or taken some $15,000 in just a year and a half, not to mention charging up Mom's credit card to the tune of $5,800. I talked to Julia about getting help, she was belligerent and refused any. So, the last thing was to get her and her belongings out of Mom's apartment. I drove her to the city with all her stuff.

After all the hoopla with Julia, Mom was on a spiral curve downward. She started showing more signs of Alzheimer's, so we told her about Board and Care. She would live in a residential setting with four to six other people. They would have separate bedrooms but would share the common areas like the living room, dining room, and kitchen. She was not altogether keen on the idea but eventually agreed that it might be easier for her to manage there. She was there about 15 months but started to go downhill quickly after about six months.

Julia's mental illness and acting out had clearly taken a toll on my mother. She said she wanted to be with my father constantly. About a month before her death, she and Jill had a conversation that she would not want to have with me. She wanted to die. She wasn't happy about her situation anymore and she missed my father. She would say repeatedly that she wanted to be with him.

She asked Jill, "How does one die? Do I have to stop walking?"

Jill answered, "Yes."

"Do I have to stop talking?"

"Yes."

"Do I have to stop drinking and eating?"

"Yes, Anna."

From then on, my mother stayed in her bed and would not or could not walk.

One morning, the staff reported that they found her walking around the kitchen. When asked why she was up, she responded, "Jake told me if I wanted to be with him, there was a portal in the northeastern corner of the kitchen."

A conversation I did have with my mother was a question I asked her one night when Jill was with me at her Board and Care.

"Mom, when you come back to visit us, how will we know it's you?" She thought about it for a long time. She was slowly coming around to the idea of Spiritualism, but she refused to let us believe she gave it any validity. With this question, she didn't seem to care though.

"Well," she began, "for you, Janet, it will be something that moves."

"Well, that's as vague as you can get, Mom." She just looked at me and smiled.

"For you, Jill, it will have something to do with water." We all smiled at each other and the subject was dropped.

About a week after my mom passed, our friend Cathy, Jill and I were watching the evening news. I was sitting across from the living room window, and out of the corner of my eye, I could see an eight by eight stain glass picture attached to the window start rocking. It was about 10 PM. It was cold and no windows were open. It didn't start out slow but just began and ended at the same speed. It did this for several minutes, then stopped just as abruptly. We all looked at each other and Jill remarked that it was obviously my mother. I nodded in agreement.

The following night again, we were watching the 10 PM news. It had been a day. The disposal in the kitchen sink leaked and so did the line from the toilet. The big news that night was of Hurricane Anna touching down in Porta Rico. Jill and I looked at each other and laughed, "Hi, Anna," Jill said.

When we brought my mother to the peninsula to live, she found a Baptist Church just down the street from her apartment. The minister creeped me out. I really couldn't put my finger on what about him I didn't like until I agreed to attend church for Easter with Mom. He was always touching the kids and asking them to hug him. He wanted everyone to hug everyone around them and say, "I love you friend." I refused. I hugged my mother. I couldn't wait to get out of there.

On the way out of the church after the service, my mother introduced me to the minister by way of telling him that I was a lesbian. She apparently was happy about it now.

She would say, "This is my daughter, she is gay. I'm straight but not narrow."

She was very proud of that, and what could I say, for years she wasn't, so I didn't stop her. Well, the creepy minister apparently did not like gays or lesbians and he refused to talk to me whenever he visited my mother in the hospital or at home.

The day my mother passed, Jill said the Baptist minister walked by her without one word. The next day, I started calling her friends to tell them about a memorial service for her. The first call was to a close friend she made when she moved to the peninsula.

"Hi, Helen, this is Virginia's daughter."

"Oh, I'm so sorry to hear about your mom passing. You used to spend a lot of time with her." "Thank you. Yes, I did."

"We're having a memorial service for her next Thursday, and I'd like it if you could come. You could say a few words if you're comfortable doing that."

"Oh, honey, there was a memorial service for her at the Baptist Church. There was a big turn-out."

"I see, did the minister put that on?"

"Yes, didn't he tell you about it?"

"No, but thanks, Helen, you take care." I hung up the phone. I didn't want to discuss it with Helen. That little asshole bible thumping pig, I thought to myself. We had a celebration of her life anyway with my friends, some of who had become Mom's friends as well.

A week before my mother passed, I called my brothers and sisters to inform them that my mother would not be here long. My oldest brother refused to even talk with me. My middle brother got on the phone but said not one word to me. When I was finished talking, he just hung up. My sister back east told me never to call her again, or she would call the police. My baby sister wanted to come out and stay 24/7 with my mother. I told her to pick a couple of times on a couple of days. I was frankly floored by my sib's reactions, which were clearly intended to tell me how upset they were with me. They were not concerned in the least that my mother was dying, nor were they concerned about coming out to say goodbye or even to grieve together. This family was crazy.

The only person who was interested was my nephew Ben, who would visit Mom every six months when he was in school and still visited his grandmother once a year when he was out of school and was actually quite close to her. The family had turned against him as well. My sister fabricated stories about her son after he ran away from home at 16 with his older brother and refused to go back. Ben eventually became an emancipated minor.

I called Ben in Wisconsin and told him that his grandmother was very close to dying. He, his partner Jess, and their one-year old little girl were standing in his grandmother's room the next day to say goodbye. This was August 28th. Mom knew he would come. She was waiting for him to arrive. Three days after they left, his grandmother left this world.

On the day my mother died, I had shoulder surgery. I have Parkinson's and was falling constantly. On a trip to take my mother to tea, my nephew and I stepped up on the sidewalk and I suddenly noticed the sidewalk coming at me! I had seconds to decide if I wanted to land on my shoulder or my wrists, I chose my shoulder. In another few months, I would choose my wrists. But at this moment, I broke my shoulder in a couple of places.

Mom was close to death. She went into a coma after Ben left with his family. Hospice called to warn us that it could happen any time. The following day, I had shoulder surgery scheduled, so Jill offered to go over to be with her. The night before, I decided to sit with my mom. I got to the Board and Care about 8 PM. I knocked on the door and one of the staff answered. The residents were all in their rooms and the staff was down stairs getting ready to turn in.

I walked to my mother's room and quietly opened the door and peeked in. She was perfectly still, as she had been most of the week, and her blanket was pulled up to her arms and the covers were carefully folded down at that point. Her arms were by her side, outside the covers.

I sat on the side of the bed and took her hand in mine and pressed my other hand over the top of it. I sat like this for a few minutes, thinking how different she had become in her old age. She was so difficult to get along with when I was younger. Yet in her old age, she was patient and kind and not hard to get along with at all. Though her dementia could and did take us to a few strange places. I shook my head at the contrast.

I sat there with her about 45 minutes. I leaned forward and whispered in her ear.

"Mama, I forgive you everything."

Seconds passed and her eyes opened and she raised her head and smiled as she said, "And I forgive you for everything!"

To say that I was stunned would be under reporting the incident, but to say that I was totally blown away and maybe just a little scared would be more accurate. Then my mother laid her head back down, closed her eyes, and disappeared into her coma again.

I've always heard that the hearing is the last of your senses to go. My mother and I talked about everything in the latter part of her life. We, in fact, covered as much as a mother and daughter can work out, and when my mother left this earth, I felt good about our efforts.

After release from the hospital, I was still groggy when Jill dropped me at our house, where our friend Cathy was waiting to keep me company. Jill and I both felt that my mother would pass soon in the next day or so. Jill would go to my mom's today because I would be fresh out of surgery. In addition, my mother had asked that I not be there when she passed, as if she were trying to protect me from that. So, Jill graciously offered to go be with her.

I felt antsy, got up, and walked to the kitchen and leaned on the warm stove. I looked up and saw the clock flip to 4:56.

The phone rang and Cathy hollered, "Jan, it's Jill."

As I took the phone, Jill's voice almost whispered, "Your Mom passed at 4:56, honey."

Jill, who had been with my mother as she left this plane for the next, continued, "She was very much at peace, Janet."

The mother I had managed to form a friendship with after all these years. The mother who was now kind to me and accepting of who I was and my relationship with my partner. The mother who brought me into the world and surprised me, over and over again, as we cemented our relationship as mother and daughter. The mother who watched me grow up and leave home and the mother I watched grow old was now gone. I knew I would see her again. Jill and I are spiritualists, we believe in life after life. Until then, I would have to be content knowing that my parents were with me in spirit.

I sat down across from Cathy, wishing I could be with Jill or at the very least alone. I didn't want to share my grief with Cathy. I didn't know when Jill would be back. I got up and walked to the kitchen, feeling numb. I went to the garage and started the dryer to freshen up a load of clothes but decided to leave them in there. I sat in the garage for a time that didn't feel long to me, but eventually, Jill drove up and smiled as she drove into the garage. The door shut and we met.

"I'm so sorry, sweetie," she said.

"I miss her already," I said as we held each other. We walked in the house and Cathy had gone upstairs. I picked up the phone. Jill put her arms around me and pulled me close. We sat down together. I felt tears welling up. I called Julia and Ben.

Chapter Twelve

Frost Heaves and Faeries

In 1955, my father was transferred to one of the last places in his military career before he retired. It was to Fairbanks, Alaska. When his tour was up in 1958, he decided to make the trip back to New York State, an adventure. He bought a VW bus and outfitted it with beds, a port-a-potty, two 55-gallon drums of gasoline on the roof, blankets, pillows, food, and water. He packed up his wife, two sons, and two-year old daughter and set off for this big adventure.

I'm sure that my mother did not look at this trip as an adventure but rather as a really long way to get back to upstate New York where her family was, but if it made my father happy, she was a willing participant. She was glad to be leaving Alaska. She hated it there and could never think of their home as any more than an intrusion on bear and moose country.

They had three kids now, Janet, 2, Joe, 6, and Jack, 9. My mother would tell anyone willing to listen that what made it hard was there was very little daylight in the winter months, about three hours each day, and that it was so blessed cold. Forty to sixty below was not unheard of. In the summertime, aside from growing the biggest, baddest mosquitos on earth, it had the longest days of any state in the U.S. because it was the northern most state of any in the U.S. The sun wouldn't set but just came down to the horizon and came back up. She said it severely screwed up the kid's biorhythms and could make a person go crazy.

I looked up mental illness in relation to light or lack thereof and came across an article that claimed Alaska had the highest suicide rate of any state in the U.S. due to many different things, but the one common denominator was the very short winter days. The same was true for places such as Norway, Sweden, Denmark, Russia, those countries in the very northern most latitudes.

The Alcan Highway (short for Alaska/Canada) was built during World War II. It stretched 1,700 miles in 1958 from Dawson Creek, British Columbia, to Delta Junction, Alaska. When my parents drove it in 1958, it was little more than a dirt road on a very wild landscape. In the spring, the rains made the road an unbearable mud pit. As the weather started getting colder, it would freeze the road and make it drivable again. My dad decided he would go at the beginning of winter because the ground was more stable and the bears would be in hibernation, an important consideration for someone who was in charge of a search and recovery team in Fairbanks. There were no gas stations or tourist stops of any kind.

Entertainment meant games the kids could play in the car, like "I spy" or one of my parents engaging us all in song. My mother, not the best driver in the world, helped out with the driving. My father figured she would be ok. Nervous or not, he said they didn't see any cars sometimes for hours. I didn't really understand how scary my mother's driving was until I drove up to Alaska and stopped at a place called Watson Lake, notable because that was my mother's maiden name. I called my dad.

"Dad, I'm at a place called Watson Lake."

"Oh, that's where your mother nearly took all of us over a cliff!"

"Really?" I asked.

"Really, I decided I better take over all the driving, and I was so tired by the time we arrived in at grandpa's in New York State that I slept for three days!"

My memories of this trip exist as still picture memories, like my brother Joe getting car sick right at the beginning of the trip or watching my father put the last of the fuel from one 55-gallon drum in the VW bus and then throwing the barrel down a hillside. I also remember seeing a tall piece of wooden post that held signs, and each sign pointed to a city and listed the mileage to get there. There must have been 30 signs. Today, there are hundreds! Over the years, with modern highway developments, I would have a considerably shortened route of 1,350 miles, 350 miles shorter than my father drove on the Alcan.

Some 30 years later, I decided I wanted to have my own adventure on the Alcan Highway, so I contacted a friend, Charlie Harris, to see if he was interested in joining me on this journey. We'd been good friends since we met in the work place on the local Air Force base in Rome, New York. That was 1974. He was my first choice of someone to travel with. He had a four-year old and a two-year old daughter and was married to a childhood friend of mine. I knew I wouldn't be bored and that I could trust him with my life. He was an engineer, so if there was something that needed fixing, he would be the perfect one to figure it out. The hitch with Charlie was Terry. They had been married a little over four years and so I wasn't at all confident that they were up to him taking this much time from his new family. We were planning on being away a month.

Even though Charlie and I talked about making the trip together, he hadn't given me a solid yes or no answer, so I gave him a couple of weeks to figure out if he wanted to do this. A little more than a couple of weeks had passed and I was getting worried. I was prepared to go by myself, but it certainly wouldn't have been my first choice.

Finally, after two and a half weeks, Charlie called, "Hi, love."

"Hi, Charlie."

"You sound cautious," he said.

"Do I?"

"Just a little."

"Does that mean that you aren't picking me up when you go north?"

"Yeah?"

"Yeah."

"Oh my God, Charlie, this is going to be so much fucking fun."

I heard him laugh, "I know." I was practically levitating!

"Terry says that I owe her big time and she expects to see the Amalfi coast next year!"

"That girl drives a hard bargain." We both laughed. "So, am I picking you up in Tacoma?" "Well, I'll be on a job in your neck of the woods in South City. Maybe we could swing by Tacoma so that I could see Terry and the girls and pick up my bike."

"Absolutely."

I'd purchased a Chevy Van about two weeks prior, put up black-out curtains in every window, but in the front, made a curtain that opened and closed to separate the cab from the rest of the van. I built a wooden frame to hold a queen mattress with a few wooden supports underneath and the rest of the space beneath the bed would be used for storage. I packed blankets, pillows, sheets, a backpack of towels, wash clothes, hand soap, shampoo, sun block, moisturizer, two pairs of mountain sunglasses (the kind with the sides blocked off so one's eyes are really protected from sun or snow glare). I also packed two pairs of my regular glasses. I brought warm changes of clothes, gloves, scarves, hats, jacket, long and short, and hiking boots I'd just finished breaking in.

I bought a ten-disk CD player, which Charlie was able to install. He would be staying with me for four days before we took off while he worked on the job in South City. I packed binoculars, my camera and 40 rolls of film, batteries, AAAs, AAs, Cs, Ds and 9 volts for camera, camera flash, and flashlights. I made sure I had maps for every state we would travel through and BC as well. I also had the AAA book for hotels and campsites and the book for the Chevy Van. There was a spare tire up under the end of the van, tire changing equipment, and car paraphernalia.

I packed a hunting knife, a batt, several balls and two gloves, a football, a cooler with food, fresh and frozen, that held ice but plugged into the cigarette lighter. I had a fair amount of dried and canned foods. I also loaded the Coleman stove with extra propane containers, cooking utensils, and pots and pans, dish soap, and laundry soap. I had a port-a-potty and four weeks of bags. Just for good measure, I packed a small tent, some air mattresses, an air compressor that plugged into the cigarette lighter and a foot pump, a medium size inflatable raft, anchor, and four wooden paddles. I loaded some tools, a full gas can, one extra gas can, and extra car parts.

Since there were two of us going, we attached a bike rack on the front of the van for two. I put mine on and Charlie would pick his up in Tacoma. Finally, the doctor that I used to work for gave me a gift of a pretty serious first aid kit. There were five vials of morphine, ten syringes, a bottle of Vicodin, a bottle of antibiotics, sterile bandages, tape, self-sticking wrap, saline solution, bottles of alcohol and peroxide, super glue, stretch wrap, razors, tubes, scissors, hemostat, and clear adhesive wrap. Charlie and I sat down one evening and pulled out the pot that my brother gave me and rolled ten neatly wrapped joints. We packed them in test tubes surrounded by cinnamon. We also secured a stretcher that we strapped to the roof. Charlie said he was bringing a high-powered rifle and his service revolver and ammo for both. He insisted that we get to a gun range so that I was experienced on both, which we did two days before we left. He endeared himself to my father with that. My father's contribution was a suggestion to bring fishing gear for some of the best salmon fishing in the world, so we did.

I had two cocker spaniels, Roo and Matilda, or Tilly as we called her. They were coming on the trip as well, so was their food, beds, toys, and odd supplies for them. Each had an appointment to clear them for travel and make sure their shots were up to date. Tilly had just finished her first heat the morning of June 2nd, 1988. Charlie and I rose at 6 AM, had breakfast, cleaned up, turned off the appliances, made a final sweep for things to take, locked the doors, drove to the local gas station, checked the oil, gassed up the "heavy Chevy," as she was dubbed by friends, gave the pups a bone, and took off for the land of the "midnight sun."

Because we got an early start, we made it to Northern California and decided we would stay in a town called Weed. I'd been there before on our way to Crater and Diamond Lakes. We pulled off the beaten path on a dirt road with Mount Shasta in full view. She was spectacular. I took the dogs out for a walk, took some pictures, and went back to the van to make my first entry in my trip journal.

We spent some time in Oregon driving to Crater Lake. Although we were anxious to hit the Alcan and start our journey north, we both wanted to spend time, mesmerized by the site of Shasta and Crater Lake, which is one of planet earth's jewels. It's an ancient volcano that looks like it erupted straight into the atmosphere. When you first glimpse this massive crater, it's from high above and a path takes you down to the water front. On the way down, if you run your hands along the dirt wall, you will feel loads of pumice, a hallmark stone of volcanic eruption. When you reach the bottom of the path, you look at the crystal-clear water and it looks to be only a few feet deep because it's so clear, but the reality is you're looking at water that is 50 feet deep! The only thing that is allowed in the water is the Ranger's boat and sulfur floating on the surface from the original volcanic blast.

We leashed up the dogs and hiked around the base of the volcano and then made our way to the top again. We took some more pictures and pulled into a camp site nearer to Diamond Lake to strategize about our trip for the next couple of days driving. We woke to a huge snow storm. Everything was covered and it was coming down hard. We ate a quick cereal breakfast and got on the road. Driving was horrible, we were only inching along. I had chains, but

I truly believed we would be out of the snow in short order. Any speed I picked up made the van slip and slide. Now there was no place to pull over.

Charlie and I were a little nervous, until Charlie said, "Jan, we're in no hurry; if the road is bad, let's just get to a place where we can stop and put the chains on."

A few minutes later, we came out of the mysterious snow storm and the road was dry again.

"That was weird," said Charlie. It was June and very cold. As soon as we left Crater Lake, the weather turned warmer. We got a late start due to the snow storm, so we decided to take our time and go directly to Tacoma, pulling into Charlie's driveway in early evening. Terry had dinner waiting for us and their two little girls gave their father a delightful hello. Since they had no pets other than gold fish, Roo and Tilly were joyfully welcomed into the household for the night.

In the morning, Charlie brought his very full backpack, guns and ammo, and some additional fishing gear to pack in the van. Kate called about two months before to get the particulars so that she could arrange a visit with her family and rendezvous with Charlie and I. Terry called Kate to tell her when Charlie and I would be in Vancouver. Kate excitedly told Terry that she and Elspeth would be in Vancouver to meet us. Charlie and I were just as excited to be spending time with them.

Charlie and Terry said a very long goodbye while I loaded the dogs. He took both his daughters on his knees and hugged and kissed them and talked very softly and lovingly to them. Terry and I hugged.

"Take good care of yourself, Jan. And take care of him!" she smiled. Charlie was the first to drive, and off we went.

"What's the mileage to Vancouver?" I asked Charlie.

"176 miles. Do you know the name of their hotel?" he asked.

"Yeah, it's the Fairmont Waterfront Hotel."

"I know that place," said Charlie. "It's right near the ferries going north on the Alcan."

We had arranged to meet them in the lobby. We parked in the hotel lot and walked in. Kate was sitting and talking to Elspeth. She looked regal. When she saw us, she took Elspeth's hand and got up, fairly dragging her. Elspeth unhooked her hand from Kate's grasp and Kate ran to Charlie and me, hugging us both. Kate was wearing slacks that were very girlish and a very low-cut top with her jacket open. It was hard for Charlie and me not to notice, the cleavage bouncing when she ran. She was always so sexy and here I was in jeans, a thermal henley, flannel shirt, and shit-kicker boots. Everybody kissed and said hello.

"Kate, I've missed you!"

"Me too," she said, smiling. When Elspeth caught up to us, we gave her hugs and hellos as well. "You look like the cat that ate the canary," Charlie said, smiling. "We have so much to tell you." Elspeth knew a café up the street within walking distance and so we went there for some lunch. We chit chatted about everything under the sun, work, vacations, families. Kate had been to Arizona to visit Justine and Tanya, Mindy lived near her father in Quincy, Massachusetts. Dawn lived in Utah. Kate was upset that no one in the family was able to break through Dawn's Mormon barrier She had two boys, and she did keep contact with the family but on a very sterile basis. Their father was very unhappy with Dawn's situation.

Justine was divorced and remarried. She had one son and he looked just like her.

Kate said, "His name is Jack. Did you know that she named him after your brother?"

"My brother?" I was shocked.

"Apparently she had a terrible crush on your oldest brother Jack."

"Oh my God, I've been in touch with Justine for years, she never told me that."

"Justine can be such a surprise at times," said Kate.

Elspeth was sweet and happy to be meeting Kate's family.

"What do you think of this group of Hart's," Charlie asked.

"They're all so kind."

"They are," I said. "Kind to a fault," and I smiled. "Is this your first trip to the states?"

"Yes," Elspeth replied. "It's so beautiful." Then Kate caught us up with her and Elspeth's news. "We bought an old farm in Bruges, Belgium."

The girls and Charlie chatted about the farm. They even had animals, goats, chickens, and horses.

"Who is taking care of your animals?" I asked.

"My brother," said Elspeth. "He is going to school and stays there because it's closer than my parent's home and takes good care of all the animals."

Charlie leaned forward to say, "Jan's covered wagon is parked outside."

"Oh," said Kate, "I can't wait to see it," as she rubbed her hands together.

Kate and I walked arm in arm behind Charlie and Elspeth from the café to the parking lot.

Kate leaned into me and said, "Do you think that you will be able to come and visit Elspeth and me at our farm?"

"I'd like to. You know, Kate," I said, "I didn't actually think that you would stay in Europe after you finished school." Kate smiled.

"I know my father and sisters thought I would come back to the states as well. But I love it there, Jan, and I've been there for so long that it feels comfortable to me."

"You know you have a bit of an accent, Kate?"

"Yes, I'm told that."

"It's really quite charming," I said. She just smiled. "The last time I saw you, Kate."

I stopped wondering if I should say it. She waited for me to finish. "I thought that you and I…" "Oh, Jan, when I met Elspeth, we were very casual with one another. I didn't expect to fall in love, it just happened."

"That's usually how it goes," I said.

At some point, we stopped walking and just stood face to face talking very softly.

"Honestly, Kate, I understand, I am happy for you and disappointed for me."

"I've loved you for a long time, Jan. I hope you will stay in our lives and I will tell you what I told Elspeth. I have two women in my life who love me, and it makes me feel very lucky. They are both smart, loving, kind, strong, independent, and adventurous women. I ask that you both use your attributes with each other and realize how much you have in common. I love you both very much. Please promise me that you will try and understand what I just told you and that you will visit us."

"I will."

"Good, let's catch up with those two."

Charlie was watching Kate and I intensely. As we started to walk again to the van, he haltingly turned to Elspeth and opened the slider, so the dogs could greet us, tails wagging.

"Oh, they are so cute," said Elspeth.

Kate stood slightly in back of Elspeth but ahead of Charlie and agreed with Elspeth that the dogs were cute. Kate grabbed my arm and held it.

Charlie showed the girls the back and said, "Jan built the bed frame with the storage beneath."

I dropped my arm from hers, but she reached for it again and held on to it. "Jan, did you do all this?"

"Well, Charlie helped; he put in the sound system and helped me get things together."

Elspeth was still looking under the bed at the storage and Kate pulled my arm, drawing me to her and whispered in my ear, "You're full of surprises," and kissed me on the cheek.

Charlie was standing at the van, talking to Elspeth about the storage. While Elspeth was still bent over looking at the underside of the bed, he had one eye on Kate and me, and she grabbed me and hugged me tight.

Charlie's raised his eyebrows as Kate whispered in my ear, "I love you, Janet Jacobs."

Kate took my arm again and we all stood there in the wet, cold weather, motionless for a moment. Charlie looked at his watch and remarked.

"If you want to catch the ferry love, we should probably get going."

He said a very loud goodbye to Elspeth and then a very quiet goodbye to Kate. The girls stood on my side of the van, Elspeth waved, Kate put her hand on the open window, and for a moment, looked sad, but only for a moment then, she put her hand on her heart and mouthed the words, "I love you, my heart misses you." I felt as if I had just had my heart torn out but then I felt like that every time I said goodbye to Kate.

We drove in complete silence to the ferry terminal, got in line, and put the car in a spot below. We set the dogs up with food and water, grabbed our coats, scarves, and gloves and walked to the aft part of the main deck. We stood at the railing side by side, leaning into one another.

"You want to talk about what happened back there?"

"No, not really."

"Well, it looked to me like the two of you were having a moment."

"That's absolutely true. Charlie, can we just forget about it now? I will tell you about it sometime later?"

"Sure." He put his arm around my shoulders and I cried very softly.

The ferry ride through the inside passage was spectacular. Neither Charlie nor I felt like talking much, but we enjoyed the scenery together. We were two days on the ferry and we saw one very beautiful sunset and a spectacular sunrise the following morning. We got very little sleep because we were checking on the dogs a lot. We took turns feeding and exercising them. By 9 AM, the ferry was slowing to pull into the terminal. We went below and prepared to fall in line and pull off the ferry.

The ferry delivered us to Juneau, Alaska. I planned to stay there one day, but we stayed three. My first order of business, there was a trip to the office of vital statistics to pick up a birth and death certificate for Virginia Anne, my parents third baby who died because her lungs were not developed. Having completed that we broke out the bikes and took a ride around the city to look at the local architecture, which had a heavy Russian influence. The buildings were unique and I found myself taking tons of pictures, hoping to do paintings when I got back home. We took a trip to the Mendenhall Glacier. It was a brilliant blue color. We were able to take a walking path beside it, allowing us to see how vast and impressive it was.

We had to get back on the ferry to go to Skagway from Juneau. The dogs had been cooperative, and we thought we'd spend a long day and night resting and paying attention to them. In the afternoon, we arrived in Skagway, 1,541 miles from Vancouver, B.C.

We went to town, which was like an old western village. I walked with Tilly, who loved to be with people, and Roo walked with Charlie. Charlie's extremely good looks and the cuddly looking dog beside him made him an instant "babe magnet."

Charlie and I started talking with folks who had a handle on where to go to give the dogs exercise. People seemed to agree that the field about two miles back was an excellent place to run the pups. We were warned to keep an eye out for moose because they would charge the dogs. One guy said the field at the edge of the woods was a spot where bears foraged and to be careful.

The field was huge about two football fields long. You could see any wildlife approaching from a distance. We let the dogs loose and watched as they played and ran, making up for the boring ride of the last couple of days. We sat in the opening of the sliding door, thinking this was a great idea, and then as if a bomb went off in front of us at the same time, we saw it. The very distinct coloring and massive size of an Alaskan Brown Bear, a fierce animal that could kill you in one blow.

"Charlie, is that a…"

"Jesus," Charlie said as he hopped to his feet and ran to the back of the van for the rifle.

"Yes, it is."

"Call the dogs, Jan, get them in the car, now!" I could hear Charlie digging under the bed for his ammo.

"Call the dogs, Jan, get them in the van! Hurry."

My heart was pounding as I hollered and whistled for them.

"Shit."

I could hear him trying to load the rifle and fumbling.

"Get the dogs in the car, Jan."

I continued to call the dogs and was screaming for them now. He lifted the rifle so that he was looking out the scope. The dogs were on their way back and out of the woods, when on the opposite side of the field, appeared two cubs. This was a mother bear, and when she caught sight of the dogs between she and her cubs, she perceived them to be a threat. She was now in full charge toward Roo. Roo and Tilly were running to the van at a good clip when Roo spotted the mother running toward him. He stopped and began barking. I was in such a panic that I began to scream and run at him. Charlie came up in back of me, grabbing my arm and swinging me in the opposite direction.

"Get in the van, now, go."

Tilly had reached me and I picked her up and ran to the van. I leashed her to the bed frame and closed all the doors but the passenger side, got in the driver's seat, and started the van. Charlie was whistling these earsplitting whistles that finally got Roo's attention and he began running toward Charlie. When Roo got close enough, Charlie grabbed him and practically threw him into the Chevy and followed, slamming the door.

"DRIVE, DRIVE!" screamed Charlie.

When I looked in the rear view, the bear was maybe 20 feet behind us and closing in quickly. "Shit," said Charlie.

We bumped violently off the field and that damn bear was still in pursuit! When we hit the blacktop, I gunned it and we took off.

Somewhere I remember reading that there was really no way to escape an Alaskan Brown Bear, that if they wanted to kill you they could. They can swim, climb trees, and could run in a burst of speed about 30 miles an hour.

"Jesus Christ! That's about as close as I've come to shitting my pants!" said Charlie.

"Welcome to the Tundra," I said while trying to shake off my own fear melt down. We were both ready for a beer.

"Let's head back into town," he said.

We did and I sussed out a camp ground with the locals while Charlie stayed with the dogs and van. I got directions for a good spot and walked back to the van to see Charlie, narrating our story of the afternoon to a small crowd, Roo and Tilly reveling in the attention. Here's my brave wife now, the girl who saved my life.

I smiled and said, "Let's go set up camp, dear."

"Ok, babycakes!" I laughed and got in the van.

All the guys were giving him high fives.

"Take care, Charlie."

"Babycakes?!" I said. He laughed.

We drove to the campground, pulled out the Coleman, made some biscuits, and heated some beans and sausages and pulled out a couple of cold beers. We gave the dogs their food, but they were more interested in our faire, so we gave them a little of ours as well. We sat around the fire, which was weird because it never really got dark. We caught up on news and laughed at stories, Charlie talked about his girls. Marta, the four-year old, who was quite a talker. She had a favorite word that she used frequently, it was "lasterday," which was a replacement for yesterday. I chuckled, but it made sense to me. It was the last day before today. Charlie said Kyle, the six-year old, had expressed frustration that Marta was always bothering her. She was told she needed to be patient with her little sister, but when the grandparents came to pick up Marta for a weekend visit, Kyle asked if they could please keep her four-year old sister until she was six!

Charlie and I shared a lot of laughs. We talked about the bear incident with as much chill and fear as we had that afternoon. We talked about driving plans for tomorrow. We were headed to Valdez. It was 708 miles, so it would take a couple of days. By 9 PM, the dogs, Charlie and I were hunkered down in the "heavy Chevy." Good idea Love to put up black-out curtains. Even though it was after 9 PM, the sun was still pretty high in the sky. Since it was getting to be the middle of June, we were looking at the longest day of the year, so the sun wouldn't even set; it would just come down to the horizon and rise again.

I crawled into bed and turned on my side, fluffing my pillows.

"I'm tired," I said.

Charlie crawled in next to me and the dogs settled in at our feet. Charlie rolled off his back and on to the same side as me and nestled up close and threw his arm over me.

"I love you my friend," he said.

"I love you, too, Charlie."

Nothing about this made me feel uncomfortable, we'd established years ago that I liked and loved women, and Charlie was married with two kids, so his hugging me represented just a love between friends. Seconds later, I heard him snoring. I drifted off to sleep.

When I awoke, I heard Charlie singing, "another Saturday night and I ain't got nobody, I got some money, cause I just got paid, oh how I wish I had someone to talk to, I'm in an awful way….."

"Good morning, love."

"Good morning, Charlie."

"I got eggs, toast, potatoes, and coffee."

"You're amazing, Charles."

The dogs were pretty sedate, so I knew they had been walked and fed.

"Thank you for taking care of the beasties."

"You're most welcome, love."

I ate my breakfast and made a run to the shower. We packed up the Chevy and got on the road. While Charlie got behind the wheel, I kicked off my shoes and put my feet on the dash. The dogs came into the cab and wanted attention. Cat Stevens was playing on the CD player. Before leaving Skagway, we took some pictures of the beautiful landscapes. I closed my eyes and sang with Charlie and Cat Stevens. The sun felt good on my body and the air was crisp and cool.

On the road to Valdez, the country kept getting more and more incredible with snow covered mountains and valleys awash with beautiful shades of brown and blue and green. You need not wonder where the inspiration for all the beautiful paintings came from if the artist even glimpsed this landscape. More than once we stopped the van just to take pictures because there just weren't adequate words to describe all this to someone who never saw such beauty we had been so lucky to see.

Charlie wanted to drive for a long time. The two of us normally switched off every three to four hours. However, Charlie had been at it five and a half hours and didn't give the appearance of someone wanting to give up soon.

"Hey, Mr. Harris, you working something out?"

"I talked with Terry last night."

"Is everything alright at home?"

"Yes," he said, smiling. "I'm going to be a father again."

"Nooooo, really? That's wonderful!"

"It t'is, thanks." He was looking almost shy.

Charlie's thing was that every child was conceived on a special occasion.

"What was the occasion? Must have been St. Patty's Day," I chuckled, Charlie smiled.

Of the 708 miles from Skagway to Valdez, we knocked down 450, so we had only 285 miles left to go. We decided to stop in one of the overnight places. They had gas and groceries, showers, car, RV, and big rig washes. We were grateful for all their amenities. The van was filthy. We over heard a few conversations about driving: That the closer you got to Valdez, the more road construction you ran into, but it really wasn't too bad, it slowed traffic only a little.

The next morning seemed easier than the ones we had been having, mainly because the smell of pancakes, bacon, and maple syrup came wafting out of the café, and it was a given that we would partake. To heck with the stuff in the fridge! We walked the dogs and fed them first and let them rest in the van.

After breakfast, we went to the souvenir shop, checked the oil on the heavy Chevy, gassed it up, and pumped quarters into the soap and water sprayer, taking off a few layers of dirt, then we took off for Valdez.

Valdez is an interesting place. We arrived about three in the afternoon. We drove down to the waterfront, which is where the city of Valdez used to be, but after the earthquake of 1964 and the tsunami that followed, it was determined that Valdez was at such great risk for future earthquakes and resulting tsunamis that the city was moved away from the waterfront to higher ground. The earthquake in 1964 was 9.2, the highest ever recorded in the United States and the second largest in the world. It was found that the epicenter of the quake was College Fjord in Prince William Sound. Valdez is also home to Columbia Glacier, the second largest tidewater glacier in North America.

Valdez would be our first stop of any length to give us a chance to rest a bit from all the driving. We decided to camp at Fielding Lake Recreation Area. Fortunately, we were near a shower/restroom and didn't have to get too primitive with the port-a-potty. We decided the first thing we wanted to do was to take the dogs with us for a hike. All of us had been cooped up in the van for way too long. We put backpacks on the dogs and put water bottles and treats in them. In our backpacks, we carried water for us, snacks, an extra sweater, and a few medical supplies. We talked to a few fellow campers, who told us the best place to hike and off we went, being pleasantly surprised by a suspension bridge on the hiking path. There were no worries about getting back by dark because it wouldn't really get dark at all. We got the word of a baseball game that was played every night starting at 10 PM.

When we returned to the camp sight, it was 11 PM and we were hungry. We cooked up some steaks, potatoes, and broke open a couple of beers. Afterward, we sat at the picnic table with the dogs and just watched as a sizeable fire died down.

The following morning, we woke a little later than usual. The dogs were as happy as we were to do nothing, or maybe they just enjoyed being with us. Whatever their motives, it was a lazy morning. We got up, took showers, and Charlie cooked some English muffins with ham, spinach, poached eggs, and hollandaise sauce. There was orange juice and coffee as well.

"This is excellent, Charlie."

"What would you like to do today, love?"

"Well, I have this idea…"

"Yes?"

"I saw a doggie day care center and I also saw a boat trip to Prince William Sound. What about doing that? The dogs won't have to be cooped up. They can play and we get a fabulous boat trip.

We have to get up pretty early to get the pups to the day care and for us to get on the train."

"Is the dog care place open that early, love?"

"Yes, it caters to the tourists who are taking trips to places like Prince William Sound."

"Sounds fun," he agreed.

So the following morning, we got up about 4 AM and took the pups to Doggie Day Care, then went to the train station, where we left at 5 AM to board the train for Prince William Sound.

Prince William Sound was absolutely gorgeous. The water was a beautiful blue/green, and all the glaciers around it were the same color as well. Even though the day was warm, we were advised to dress warmly for the day. For-tunately, we listened to that piece of advice. For while the sun was shining and the temperature was 72, we were in a valley of ice. It was like being a cherry floating in a bowl of ice cream! We spent the day there, the trip providing lunch. We watched as calving took place, always spectacular to watch. The other and probably most wonderful thing about the Sound was the wild life. In that one day, we saw puffins, sea otters, porpoise, harbor seals, bald eagles, a humpback whale and baby, common murro, flying back and forth to their nests on the cliffsides, sea lions and a minke whale; we saw so many birds that I had to take pictures and look them up when I got back to the van to know what they were. Prince William Sound was teaming with life.

Little did we know that the following year in 1989, the oil tanker, the Exxon Valdez, would change life as Alaskans knew it. The tanker would destroy the lovely Prince William Sound and the coastal area in and around Valdez. The oil spill would ravage the pristine waters, coating beaches in oil sludge and killing thousands upon thousands of wildlife. We learned that oil has a life that far ex-ceeds the life of a beautiful sound or beach or bay. That oil would be cleaned and gathered as best as we humans could, but it would never go away; it would always remain beneath the water. Things would never be the same, ever again.

By late afternoon, the sun wasn't warming up enough. It was getting very cold. We headed back to port and our pups. We were tired. We picked up the dogs and went back to camp. We fired up the Coleman and ate beans and hot dogs. I fed the dogs and we laid on the bed in the van facing out the back door, look-ing at the fire while we ate.

"Maybe the dogs can visit with their friends tomorrow," said Charlie, "and we can go kayaking." "Ok with me." I had a minor reservation about deserting the dogs for another day, but they seemed ok.

Charlie and our camping neighbor had been talking and decided to go for a run first thing in the morning. He took the dogs with him and they all seemed quite content when they returned. I was happy to hang out at camp and fill in my journal. Just after lunch, we dropped the dogs to day care and headed down the hill. We rented a couple of kayaks and paddled around the glaciers in the bay. It was truly calming as we glided through the water. I'd never have thought to do this if Charlie had not suggested it. After about three hours, we came back to the small bay and paddled back to the rental place.

After five enjoyable days in Valdez, it was time to hit the road again. We packed up and gassed up. I climbed into the driver's seat, and Charlie put on some Jackson Browne and we sang to the "pretenders." We made several stops to take in the Chugach Mountains. As we drove through canyons, we spotted mountain goats comfortably hoofing along a shear drop. The mountains were indeed majestic and stunning, the highest peak being Mount Baker at 13,094 feet. We were headed north again to Anchorage and Denali National Park, where Mount McKinley would break the record for the highest peak in the nation, at 20,320 feet.

Anchorage was 154 miles north of Valdez. It's a thriving metropolis.

"It's Alaska's largest city, did you know that, Mr. Harris?"

"I did, love."

"Here's one I bet you don't know, Charles. It's the 4th largest city in the U.S. by land area at 1,961 square miles, nearly the size of Delaware."

"I didn't know that," said Charlie.

"Here's one for you, love. How many mountain ranges can you see on a clear day from Anchorage? If you get it wrong, you'll have to shed an article of clothing."

"Oh, we're playin this shit again, are we?"

"Don't be a sore loser!"

"Ok ,go."

"The Chugach, the Kenai, the Talkeetna, the Tordrello, the Alaskan, and the Aleutian."

"Right!"

"Charlie, this says that 250 black bears and 60 Grizzlies live within urban Anchorage. They also say that the Iditarod starts on the first Saturday in March with the ceremonial send off in downtown Anchorage. Do you know what the ending point is?"

"I believe it's Nome."

"Right you are, Mr. Harris!"

"What does it say about population?" Charlie wanted to know. "It says that in 1940 the population was 4,000, and in 1988, it was 300,000!"

About mid-afternoon, we rolled into down town Anchorage. The weather was warm and delightful.

"Where should we go first?" Charlie asked.

The dogs were demanding our attention, so we discovered a dog park off 32nd St. We let the dogs out and they ran and played for more than an hour.

When the dogs had been run, peed, popped, and fed they settled down in the Chevy for a nap, so we went for a summer time ride on the Iditarod trail. We located the place and a large wheeled cart was attached to the dogs. It held a bunch of people, but there were only four others riding with Charlie and me. Since the dogs were settled in the van, we decided to take in another activity that we wouldn't be able to do if we had the dogs with us, so we went to Kincaid Wild Life Park. It was an area where one could get deep into the woods to view wildlife. It was home to Alaska's largest moose population.

By the time we set up camp, we were beyond tired. We ate cereal and crawled in the bed. Charlie was first in and stretched out his arms to welcome me and pull me in close. We laid on our sides and he held me tight. We laid like that for several minutes and he took his hand and rubbed my forehead, pushing my hair back.

"Have you talked to Terry today?"

"This morning."

"Everything ok?"

"Yes."

"Charlie, do you remember when you and Terry were dating?"

"Yeees."

"I remember that you had a guitar you used to play for her. What ever happened to that?"

"It got damaged around that time and I haven't bothered to get another."

"That's sad, Charlie, because you are so good."

"Thank you, love."

"By the way, I have a question for you; why is it you never played for me?"

"Hummm? Don't know, I'll have to rectify that."

"I'll hold you to it." Seconds later and he was snoring softly.

The following morning, I awoke by myself. I could hear Charlie outside doing something. I crawled out of bed and went outside. Charlie was bent over, standing by the picnic table, holding his hand and squeezing it, rubbing it really hard. In front of him on the ground was a broken mug of coffee.

"Charlie, you ok?"

"I'm fine, love."

"What's going on?"

"Oh, I got this wicked cramp in my hand and I let go of the mug. Sorry about the mug, you just bought it."

"Don't worry about it, I'll get another."

I sat at the picnic table.

"I'm going to shower this morning."

"Hang on, love, I'll alert the media." I chuckled.

He was trying hard to be funny, trying to cover something.

"What's our plan for the day, Charlie?" The dogs jumped up beside me on the table.

"How about something sedate today, and we'll do Matanuska tomorrow?"

"Sounds ok to me. Are you feeling ok?" I asked.

"Sure, I'm just a little tired, that's all."

"What's the sedate part you were thinking about?"

"Alaska's National Heritage Center." So, we started with the Heritage Center. They had some traditional crafts, baskets, jewelry, tools, clothes, boats, and houses of the area's indigenous people. It was really interesting.

The next day, we found a doggie day care for the pups and we went to Matanuska Glacial Experience. This was a trip through a 10,000-year-old glacial crevasse and blue water pools. It was really different to stand under a glacier, even if it was at the edge. You could almost imagine what it would look like to fall into a crevasse. It felt a little unnerving, but it was one of the most interesting things the two of us had seen. We planned to go to Chilikoot Charlie's, an unusual bar in Anchorage, but neither of us were up to it. Anchorage was definitely a fun place that held a lot of history. The end of our stay in Anchorage saw us really tired and spent again. Hopefully Denali would wake the dead in us.

Mount McKinley, or Denali, as it is now known is 124 miles north of Anchorage. Mount McKinley's name was changed in 1975 to Denali (meaning tall one). Denali is growing by .04 inches per year. Its located deep in Alaska's interior on over 6 million acres of preserved wilderness that includes massive expanses of forest, glacial lakes, frozen tundra, and towering mountains. Coming into the campground, we passed a view of the tundra and hundreds of caribou grazing in the sun. We pulled into a place called Wonder Lake Campground because it was the most remote and we thought it would cut down on the tourist riff raff. It did and we were mesmerized with beauty all around us. We spent three days in Denali Park hiking, fishing, exploring glaciers and wild life. One night, we woke to a black bear foraging the campsite, looking for food. Nothing came of it. He didn't find anything. On an afternoon hike, we came across a moose; he took notice of us, snorted a couple of times, and charged us. We were safe, hiding behind a tree, and since moose are notoriously near sighted, he lost interest pretty quickly.

The northern most city that we would visit was Fairbanks. Almost as soon as we got on the road, we had to slow for some construction. While they had a bunch of machines working on the black top, it looked to us as though the new stuff was already down and it didn't appear as though it would hold us up much, if at all. After about 15 minutes of driving, it was clear to us that the roads were in working order, and so we popped some CDs in the player, put the dogs on the bed with a bone so they could doze in comfort, and settled in for our ride to Fairbanks.

After about ½ an hour on the road, the lines on the road were vacant. It was just blacktop with no markings at all. I was doing 75 mph and had this sudden trepidation that my speed was too fast. I couldn't put things together at first, but I began to slow and got to about 60 mph and it felt like we were airborne! I continued to hit the brakes and saw the bicycles on the front of the van come up to the height of the windshield and bang on the hood and disappear, crashing into the grill and then sounding like they were tearing the undercarriage of the van off. In my peripheral vision, I could see Charlie hanging on for dear life and CDs just shooting out of the player. I hadn't realized it, but I had practically stood on the brake pedal and the van skidded sideways for several feet. We were on our half of the road and we both checked the dogs and then each other. The dogs were clearly traumatized and were shaking and on the floor. We tried to comfort them and placed them on the bed again.

Charlie looked at me and said, "What the hell just happened?"

"I dunno."

We opened the slider and went outside to look at the destruction. The bikes were bent and broken like toothpicks. They were partially under the front, and we had to back the van up in order to free them. They were a total loss. We set them on the side of the road to load on the roof to dump them in Fairbanks. The bumper was scratched and dented. The tires seemed ok, and Charlie crawled under the van to make sure nothing was punctured and leaking our engine fluids all over. Things were intact there. The only other thing that was worrisome was a small crack in the windshield on the passenger side. Both of us were trying to figure out what had just taken place when an SUV saw us and stopped.

A young couple rolled down their window, "You folks alright?"

"Yeah, yeah, we're fine," said Charlie.

"You hit a frost heave?"

"What's that?" Charlie inquired.

"It's a dip in the road caused by the permafrost melting. It happens on the roads when they put the blacktop on."

"Oh, those dips that you can see with the lines on the road?"

"Right. You have to be careful when you get to a fresh road that doesn't have the lines on it yet." "Thanks for the info," said Charlie.

"You sure you're ok?"

"We're good," said Charlie. "Thanks for stopping."

I watched them drive away then Charlie and I looked at each other.

"Let's get the bikes on the roof to dump in Fairbanks," I said.

"Would you like me to drive now?" Charlie inquired.

"Yes, yes I would."

We got back in the Chevy and put things back together. If they weren't tied down, they went flying. Fortunately, the CD player still worked. Charlie was cautious and taking things slow. After an hour or so, the road had yellow lines again to navigate by.

Fairbanks, Alaska was the place of my birth in 1956! I wanted to see everything, the hospital where I was born, where my parents lived, where my father worked, the airport he flew out of and into, the gym where he taught my brothers to box, the pool where the three of us played, my brother's school. I took in downtown and went to the Fairbanks museum showing the conception of Fairbanks. They had a micro fiche machine for back newspapers, so I looked up February 1956. I didn't find any birth announcement on the 7th, the day of my birth, but found it on the 8th of February. The announcement read: To Senior Master Sergeant C.E. Jacobs and Mrs. Charles Jacobs, a girl. Fairbanks was a time machine for me. I looked up the car dealership that kept the vehicles running 24/7 to keep the engines from freezing. My father was friends with him, and even though he would have been long retired, his son was running the business now. His father was indeed retired and living in Hawaii!

"Quite a transformation," I said. His son laughed and agreed.

The last place I was to take in on my personal tour was my sister Virginia Anne's grave. She was born March 9th, 1955, 11 months before me. She lived only two hours because she was born with holes in her lungs, not a diagnosis conducive to life in 1955. My parents told me what cemetery her grave was in, but they felt pretty certain I would not find it. After about an hour of looking, I did find it. It was a 3 x 5 piece of black plastic with "Baby Jacobs, March 9th, 1955" carved in it and glued to a cinder block. It was mud caked and I bent down to brush it free of dirt. I stood looking at it and felt a kind of dull sadness. Charlie, who had been helping me look, must have noticed my discovery. He came over to me and put his arms around my shoulders and kissed the side of my head.

"My parents must have been so incredibly heartbroken to lose her and sad to leave her behind." My eyes filled with tears.

"Let's get a picture, love, and you can get working on things. Your folks will be pleased that you're giving her a proper headstone." Now I was ready to see what we could find in Fairbanks.

Charlie and I drove over to the University of Alaska in Fairbanks. I was looking for an updated postcard to bring my dad of a grizzly bear on display that had been taxidermied more than 40 years ago. I saw the bear and then the postcards. We went to the gift store and bought a few little things. We rounded the day out by visiting Fairbanks Museum and Planetarium which was housed in what looked like an old stone church that one might see in England. We settled into a camp site but decided to go fishing on the Chena River for salmon. We took the dogs and they were as interested in the salmon as we were. We caught one that looked to be about 15 inches. Charlie cooked it up for dinner and we agreed that it was the best fish we'd ever had!

The next day, we took the dogs for a long walk. We took them with us when we visited Pioneer Park, which was kind of neat. They displayed old log cabins that were built and used in the wilderness but transported to the park when they were abandoned. The following day, we went to Alaska Botanical Gardens, which was spectacular.

We got back to the Chevy early and so decided to unwind on the bed with the pups.

We pulled out books that we brought to read and relaxed for a couple of hours, after which Charlie got up and said, "I have a surprise for you."

"Oh? For me?"

"Yes, for you."

He jumped off the bed from the back door and began rummaging around for something, then with a heave, he pulled a guitar case.

"Good grief, Charlie, what is that, a dead body? Oh my god, it's a guitar."

"That's right. I decided you had a point. I miss playing. Sometimes I get so caught up in fatherhood, work, and trying to keep Terry happy because she deserves that much. She keeps our family and home up and running, you know what I mean? She loved it when I played. I owe her the small pleasure of some music now and again, don't you think?"

"I do think, Charlie. Are you going to tell her or surprise her?"

"I thought I would surprise her. I can practice with you."

"I'd like that."

I watched as he seemed to introduce himself to the instrument and began to softly pluck the strings, the sound was pretty. Before too long, I began to recognize the melody – "Morning Has Broken." Charlie started singing and I hummed along. How calming it was to hear him play and sing. I was nearly brought to tears by the guitar and his beautiful tenor voice. After that, he played "The Journey's End," very apropos for this point in our trip.

I was happy to move on from Fairbanks. I was growing weary of traveling. Our next stop north would be to the Arctic Circle to spend the longest day of the year. It was 128 miles north of Fairbanks. We spent our last night in Fairbanks playing baseball with fellow campers, starting at 9 PM.

In the morning, we packed up and drove north to the Arctic Circle. We got there very early in the day. There wasn't much to do when we arrived, so we hung out at the van. Charlie pulled the gloves, ball, and bat out of the back.

"Come on, let's get warmed up so we can get a game going tonight."

The dogs ran back and forth while we threw the ball. We took some pictures and pulled out the Coleman to cook. We had purchased a bunch of groceries before we left Fairbanks: steak, broccoli, mushrooms, onions, potatoes, butter, ranch dressing, veggies for salad, beer, and I managed to secure a Pepperidge Farm chocolate on chocolate cake!

We walked the dogs, fed them, and played catch for a good hour or so with them.

"Charlie, you glad you came with me?"

"You bet, you're one adventurous woman, Janet Marie."

We found a place on the roadside where one could shower and generally clean up, do our laundry, and gas up the van. We made our respective phone calls to Terry and my parents. When we returned to the field, Charlie pulled out his guitar. He played and we sang, "You, who are on the road, must have a code, that you can live by...." Even the dogs loved the music. They wouldn't leave our sides when he played. "All my bags are packed, I'm ready to go, I hate to wake you up to say goodbye...."

"She never could resist a winding road, she never could resist a winding road....."

We laughed and pointed to each other.

"I'm sitting in the railroad station, got a ticket for my destination....."

People were coming to the field and parking near us. Pretty soon, there was a small contingency of RVs and campers. Every time someone parked, they would peek around the corner of our van and watch the crowd sing, joining them eventually. Before too long, there were ten or so people, then 15 and 20, standing around or bringing their chairs. This went on until we were too hungry to continue and wanted to cook our meal.

I was enjoying this so much that I whispered to Charlie, "You keep playing and I'll cook."

One couple brought their food and Coleman and asked if they could share the table with us. Another group had hot dogs and beans to share, others had pancakes, which they exchanged for some meat. They also had maple syrup! The gist of the evening was this small community of travelers gathered to see the sun that would never set. We introduced ourselves and became old friends for that one moment in time.

When we finished dinner, we shared stories and had some good laughs. At 10:00 PM, we started a game of baseball. The youngest player was eight-years-old and the oldest was 82. That night, on a permafrost field at the Arctic Circle, the world was right with everyone. No one was sad or angry, our smiles and laughter bore that out. By 11:00 PM, the bases were loaded and 82-year old Frank Culver was up to bat. He hit a good one and brought everyone home.

In the land of the midnight sun, daylight ruled. The sun came down and barely touched the horizon, then started its ascent into a brand-new day. It was pretty incredible and I figured I would probably never witness this again in my life time but here I was with my good friend, my dogs, and a bunch of people I didn't know but would always remember. We crawled into sleep about 3 AM and didn't wake until 10:00 AM. We didn't really care what time we got on the road. There were only a couple of vehicles left on the field.

Charlie wanted to drive first. I looked at the odometer; it was a little more than 4,300 miles. By the time I arrived home, it would be over 8,600 miles. I held Tilly on my lap and Roo laid down between Charlie and me. I put my sock feet on the dash and we both sang to "I never could resist a winding road, I never could resist a winding road, maybe just around a bend, a rainbow's waiting at the end, I never could resist a winding road…." We hadn't planned to stop in any particular city, just wherever we wanted to rest. It was a good trip, and I was glad to cross it off my list. I had a lot to write about but mostly I felt happy that I got to see the place where I came into the world. It was good to be on the downhill run, back to the lower 48 and home.

Chapter Thirteen

A Long Way to Fall

Deep in the heart of our neighborhood was a conglomeration of kids, rules, and hierarchies. The older kids partially ruled our world. If we measured up, that is didn't wine or cry and were tough enough, to withstand a tackle, we could be picked for all kinds of sports and games. There were times when it didn't matter and the younger kids had games of their own and the older kids were not even involved.

One of the rules was that the older kids protected all the younger ones. If a child from outside our neighborhood wanted to pick a fight with someone, usually an older kid would step in.

We had a lot of kids in our neighborhood. Our house had five, next door had two, across the street were two and next to them nine, across the street from them was five and next door to them another five, two houses down was four, down the street further was another five, and across from them three. Near us on an adjacent street was a family of five and a family of two kids. There were three homes with one kid each. Fifty kids was a lot to have, even in a big neighborhood. The amazing thing about this was that when we played together, we all got along pretty well and so did the parents with very few exceptions.

The house on the opposite corner from us had five girls when I was in sixth grade. It was the first time I fell in love – twice in one household. The girls were being raised by their father, who looked like Cary Grant. I'd watched movies and I knew Cary intimately! And here he was, living across the street from us! He was handsome and charming and gracious. He was always asking me to join them for dinner. My parents always said no, but just the fact that he always asked made me feel special.

The other crush was on one of his daughters Kate, who was two years older than I and a beauty with golden brown skin and gorgeous auburn hair. She was athletic and a strong and pretty older woman! She smoked and that made her seem very sophisticated to me.

Kate loved football, just like me. She could withstand a tackle without crying, just like me. She was very much a rebel, and I admired her for that. In the summertime, she made Vacation Bible School fun and we would memorize whole passages of verse. When VBS gave out awards for the most passages of the Bible memorized, Kate, her sisters, Justine and Dawn and I took all the awards. My dad just purchased a big, new tent for us, and my mom, who was family photographer, took a picture of all of us. When kids started to put their tents up in their backyards for the summer, everyone wanted to sleep in ours because Kate was staying with us in the new tent. Everyone loved Kate and wanted to be around her.

My friends Kerry, my age, and her older sister, Carla, and Sue and her older sister, Maggie, were the ones I hung out with. This was the first summer that Kate spent with us in the tent since her father only moved them here last September. Kate was different. She did just what she wanted in our neighborhood and what she wanted was to cruise the girls and kiss them. She did this openly with very little grief from the neighborhood. She was sexy and smart and never took shit from anyone.

Some of the boys always wanted to join us, but we never let them. In our seclusion, we played Truth or Dare and Spin the Bottle. Kate was always kissing the girls. She didn't need the excuse of a game to do it, she kissed them whenever she wanted. I found myself wanting to be around her all the time and wanted her to kiss me, too.

That evening in the tent, Sue announced to everyone, "You know Kate and Maggie sleep naked together." Kate looked at her.

"You're just jealous," Kate replied.

"No, I'm not," Sue shot back.

"I think you are," said Maggie. Sue threw a deck of cards at Maggie.

"Shut up, Maggie." Kate smiled and Maggie laughed.

I watched all of this with great interest. Kate grabbed Maggie and kissed her for a long time, and as she did, Kate's eye looked around the tent and landed on me. She stopped kissing Maggie and scooted next to me. She grabbed my shirt and planted her lips on mine. She pressed hard, and somewhere in my stomach, I had the distinct feeling of butterflies!

"You were kissing back!" Kate said as she gave me a friendly push. I said nothing but was intensely embarrassed.

"Take your clothes off."

"What? No."

"Yes, take them off, or you can sleep by yourself in your new tent." I sat there feeling really torn, but I didn't want to appear like a baby, so I took off my shirt, revealing my breasts barely there. "No bra yet?"

"I have one, I'm saving it for school." Kate laughed.

Suddenly, I felt really shy, like I wanted to run away. In my peripheral vision, I saw Kerry and Sue hug and then kiss, but they stopped to watch me.

"Come on, we've got the Playboy magazines to look at tonight," said Maggie.

"Don't be afraid," Kate said. "Take your clothes off."

"Why?"

"Because I'm going to show you what it feels like to have sex."

"I don't want to know what it feels like to have sex."

"Yes, you do, everyone does. We've all done it, and because you're doing it with a girl, there is no chance you'll get pregnant."

"Come on, you'll like it."

"I'll help you," Kate said.

"No, I can do it myself."

"Ok then...."

I looked at Kerry and she said, "It feels good, Jan, you'll like it." I slowly got to my knees and pushed my shorts down.

"No undies?" Kate asked.

"No, I went swimming earlier." It was my habit not to wear underwear after swimming,

When I was naked, Kate came over to help me.

"Here, lay on your back," and she gently helped me position. "Now tell me if this doesn't feel good."

Kate had already ditched her clothes. Carefully, she climbed on top of me. Her naked body felt soft and exciting. Kate moved ever so slightly and slid her hand down between the two of us. She pushed on herself and moaned and then pressed her fingers on me, and I found myself moving against her. I didn't know exactly what I was supposed to do or what would happen, but in those few seconds, I began to feel really good. Kate began to move faster until it seemed like she was crying.

"What's wrong," I asked her, but she just continued to sound strange and then she got off me. "Nothing's wrong, you ninny, I was having a spark."

"A spark," I repeated.

"It's what happens when you have sex. Did you have one, Jan?"

"No, I don't know."

"You'd know if you had one," said Kate.

"Come on, Kate, you can tell her about it later, let's look at the magazines."

Kerry and Carla's father was out of town on business, so they raided his collection of Playboys and brought a stack to the tent. Kate pulled on her pants and then shirt. She threw back her head and her beautiful mane of auburn hair flew back. Kerry slid over to the group to look at the magazines.

"You better hope those boys aren't hangin around our tent tonight," she said "Nobody saw or heard anything except us. Even if someone did see, no one is going to tell. We have a lot of dirt on them, and anyway, I can beat up most of them."

I decided not to think about any consequences. I'd be in a lot of trouble if anyone found out. We passed the Playboys around.

We told jokes and laughed. Maggie, Carla, and Kate had a cigarette. Eventually, everyone began to crawl into their sleeping bags and go to sleep. I lay there thinking about what Kate and I had done, unable to sleep. It seemed really bad, but it felt so good and was so exciting. I adjusted my pillow and someone yanked it out from beneath my head. It was Kate.

"Move over," she whispered. "I want to sleep with you."

I didn't say a word just slid over. I could feel her naked body and she began pulling at my shirt and shorts.

"Take them off."

I did so with the least little bit of coaxing. She pressed her body against mine and began moving like she had earlier, only now she was quiet, she barely made any sounds. We were facing each other and her hand easily searched out and found that little part of me responsible for so much pleasure. Her fingers touched and caressed everything down there until I felt like a flood gate was opening and I couldn't hold back any longer.

146

She whispered in my ear, "Did you feel your own?"

"Uh huh."

That summer night with Kate dominated everything I did for a really long time. Whenever I saw her, I made a point to be outside, so she would talk to me or ask me to join her in a baseball game. She and Maggie were clearly together and I imagined they were sleeping naked together lots. The boys followed Kate around pretty much as I did, but she wasn't the least bit interested in them. Except for my brother Joe, who she joked around with; she paid attention to the girls. She would always talk to any girl that wanted to have a conversation with her. I wondered how many other girls she slept naked with.

About a week later, Kate surprised me as I rounded the corner of my parent's house.

"Boo!"

She grabbed me and kissed me long and hard. We both smiled. She took my hand and began to swing my arm.

"I have a surprise for you."

"What?" I hated surprises.

"Well, Kerry and Carla are in Canada for a family reunion and Sue and Maggie are in New Jersey visiting friends."

"Why is that a surprise?"

"Because it means you and I are the only ones in the tent tonight." I smiled.

Kate and I had been spending more and more time together. We hung out with some of the nine kids across the street that evening. When it got dark, my dad stood at the end of the driveway and whistled for us to get ourselves home. We went in the house and got a few things we needed: a small portable T.V., some snacks, a deck of cards, a couple of pillows, and our sleeping bags. It was exciting to think we had the whole tent to ourselves.

Kate wasted no time. She pulled me to her and kissed me, and I kissed her back with wild abandon. She lifted the front of my shirt and pushed it up over my head.

"Take off your shorts," Kate urged.

She did as well. I laid down inside the sleeping bag, and Kate crawled in beside me. This would be how we spent the summer, naked and playing with each other. We became inseparable. Eventually, Maggie stopped coming around.

Kate went to the river with me. We had three days together alone before my cousins arrived. My gram doted on both of us. One of the days we went out for the whole day. We packed a blanket and some lunch and set out in the canoe for one of the small, uninhabited islands.

One evening as it was getting dark, we were playing a game of kickball. As I ran to home, I neglected to see a small metal garden fence and impaled my leg on it. I don't remember feeling any pain.

Kate came over and said, "I'm getting my dad, the fence is in your leg."

In a few minutes, my favorite two people in the whole world were kneeling over me. Mr. Hart and his beautiful daughter, Kate.

"Kate, go get something to stop the bleeding."

Kate ran inside and came out with a hankie. Mr. Hart put it around my knee and tied it. Then carried me across the street to my parents, standing in the front yard talking to a neighbor. He greeted them and explained what had happened.

"Kate, take her in the house and clean up her leg."

As we walked into the house, I turned to Kate, she smiled at me. She washed my injury and began to put iodine on it.

"Kate, I want to sleep out in the tent again." She looked at me, knowing immediately what I wanted.

"We can't, summer is over and we start school day after tomorrow."

"But, I…" She put her finger to her lips to hush me.

"We can't, now be quiet so no one will hear you." I was crushed; I wanted to be with her.

"Kate, I want to sleep in the tent one more night, just you and I."

"NO, my father won't let me sleep there any longer. We have to get ready for school, and you have to stop talking about it." She put a band aide on my leg and kissed me on the cheek. "I have to go."

The following afternoon, Mom and Dad took Joan and Julia and went next door to have coffee with the neighbors. Jack had gone to the lake. Joe and I were the only ones home. I was laying on a lawn chair in the back yard but got thirsty, so I went in for a drink of water. I walked into the dining room and there was my brother Joe, who was four years older than me, kissing Kate! His arms were holding her waist tightly and her arms were around his neck. I ran at him full tilt and surprising both of them.

148

"Ugh, Jesus, Jan!"

"I hate you both," I screamed at them.

I came at him again, swinging. He held my head away from him and I bit his arm. I heard him say, "You better go," to Kate and she ran out of the house.

Next morning, school started. Justine, Dawn, and Kate came to our door, saying they wanted to walk to school with me, so the four of us did. Dawn and Kate walked behind Justine and I. Though Kate tried several times to talk with me, I resisted. When we arrived at school, we had to check the board inside and see who our teacher was. Kate and Dawn went in and looked for all four of us. Kate came back out and walked over to me.

"Jan, I'm so sorry, you have Mrs. Hahn, she's an old witch, very mean."

I didn't see Kate much for the next week and we didn't talk, but about a week later, Dawn came over to tell me that their father had been transferred to Montauk, Long Island. And they would leave in three weeks. They were all sad because they couldn't finish the school year in Rome. Dawn also told me that Kate was especially sad because she didn't have my friendship any longer.

"I know how close you both were. It's important that you have that friendship," said Dawn.

But now I was losing her again. I thought I'd better make the best of the time I had. The next time there was a football game, I went outside to see if she was playing. She was. I walked over to Kate, grabbed her by the sweater, and kissed her hard on the lips.

She kissed me back and a boy from the other team hollered, "Come on, you lezzies, let's get this game going."

We smiled and hunkered down for the game. The same boy who called us lezzies was now holding on to Kate's shirt as she tried to run with the ball. He started swinging her around by her shirt, but she wasn't going to the ground. So, I ran for all I was worth and flattened him in the dirt. Kate took off and scored. He was obviously hurt and looked like he wanted to kill me.

He started screaming, "Jesus, you fucking lezzie."

My brother came over and offered him a hand, saying, "You can't tell me, man, that you were tackled by a girl?!"

"Fuck you and your stupid sister!" Joe turned away and started laughing.

"Nice going, Jan!" Kate came over and put her arm around my shoulders and smiled.

"Maybe playing with girls is too much for you," Kate said.

"Fuck you, bitch."

"Sorry, I don't do boys."

We all started laughing. I felt extremely cool that I could come to Kate's rescue.

When the weekend came for them to move, all five girls stayed with us overnight, so the moving van could load up the previous day. I had a queen size bed, so Justine, Kate, and Dawn slept with me and the younger girls, Mindy and Tanya, with Joan and Julia. Kate laid next to me. I turned on my side away from her and felt her arms reach around me. Justine and Dawn slept on the other side of me. There was no way to pull away from Kate with all of us in the bed together. Kate continued to hug me all night, and by morning, their father was gathering all the girls to get on the road.

Everyone hugged each other goodbye. Kate was the last to hug me goodbye. She pushed my hair back, gave me a long hug, kissed me goodbye, and hopped in the car, waving to everyone else. Everyone was filing into the house.

Joe came over to me and whispered, "I'm sorry, Jan, I didn't know, Justine told me."

I just looked straight ahead until he left and then went to my room, shut the door, and cried.

When the Hart family settled in Montauk, Justine, Dawn, Kate and I were corresponding with each other. I was finishing 7th grade while Kate was finishing 9th. She was talking about what university she would go to. I talked about how she could come for a visit next summer. Her dad didn't want her to go. He had to travel in summer and he wanted Justine, Kate, and Dawn to watch their little sisters while he was gone.

Just when it seemed like we would never be together, the summer after Kate finished 10th grade, she called to say that in a week her dad was traveling upstate and he could drop her off and pick her up in two weeks.

When she finally came for two weeks, she was eager to pick up where she left off. After greeting everyone, saying goodbye to her dad, and the obligatory conversation, we went to my room where we grabbed each other and kissed.

Summertime meant that kids were still pitching tents in the backyard, and so we did, to have some privacy that night. She'd learned a few new things, and she didn't call it "sparking" anymore. We laughed about that. I asked her where she ever learned to call an orgasm "sparking." She told me that a long time ago she was staying at a friend's house in Louisiana, and she heard her friend's mother refer to it that way because it was like having an electrical charge go through our body when you had an orgasm.

I lived for these moments with Kate. The first night, we stayed up all night. Being with her felt secretly naughty and yet very grown up and exciting. We snuck out at 3 AM and rode bikes out to Lake Delta and played in the sand. Two weeks went by fast, and before I knew it, we were issuing goodbyes to each other. Later that year, Kate's dad transferred to Phoenix, Arizona and we didn't see each other until the summer after she finished high school. In the fall, she left for Rhode Island. She had been accepted at Brown University.

We talked on the phone about twice a year, and though we hoped to get together, it wasn't to happen. During the first year, at spring break, Kate said she was going to Mexico and wouldn't be able to come to New York. It was hard to hear because I knew she probably had a new lover. I sat all spring and summer with my insecurities. We spent only a couple of long weekends together while she was at Brown. Her last year there, she and I planned to get together at my urging. I would come to her graduation.

Rather than fly, I decided to drive to Rhode Island. As I drove, I began to think about how I felt. I was chasing her. I wanted nothing more than to love her and be with her. The first was easy to do, the latter was a challenge.

Our friend Charlie said to me one time, "Jan, how long have you two been doing this thing?" "What thing?"

"Don't play dumb, all she has to do is say I would really like to see you, love, and you're there." "That's not true!"

"Yes, it is."

I knew he was right, but it really didn't matter. She made me happy, and I figured at some point in time, she would believe that I was there for her and always would be and we wouldn't have to be apart anymore. I thought about Charlie's words more than once and then I put them in the back of my mind.

Kate was meeting me in the lobby of my hotel. She looked vibrant and happy with the world. She was a tall, thin drink of water. She strolled into the hotel like she knew everyone's secrets. "Hi, Jan," she kissed me like a lover, opening her mouth and taking my lips in her mouth.

I did the same and she stopped and looked at me.

"My heart misses you," she said.

"I've missed you, too." I leaned into her. She put her hand in the small of my back and pressed hard, pulling me close to her.

"Let's go up to your room. I want to do really naughty things to you."

I had never heard her talk this way before, but I liked it. I felt confident that I had a few things to show her. In the room, I pulled out the sex toys I brought.

"Well, there's absolutely no reason to go out in the world for days!" she exclaimed.

The summer after my 19th birthday, I went to Europe to see a school chum, Janice, in Holland; after two weeks, I took the train to Germany to see a friend from the states. Charlie was in the Air Force and was stationed there almost three years ago. We worked together when he was stationed at Griffiss AFB in Rome, New York. He was an extremely handsome guy and I was totally charmed by him. We started dating but very soon discovered that we liked things better as friends, and besides, I liked girls.

Kate was a dichotomy; she had been writing me since she and her sisters moved to Long Island. She had a very full life but would tell me only very generic things about her life, always ending the letter with, "My heart misses you, love, Kate. She went to Rhode Island to attend Brown University for her law degree. When she started at Gent, she took some time away from her studies to go back to the states and take the BAR and was now a lawyer. It was hard to believe, she was just so amazing. Currently, she was working on a Ph.D in psychiatry at Ghent University in Belgium.

Kate agreed to meet me in Amsterdam. I couldn't wait to see her. I felt like I was vibrating in anticipation! I purposely arranged her visit at the end of my trip because I secretly hoped that she would ask me to stay and I would accommodate her. When I got to Amsterdam, I went to the Athenum Bookstore where I was to meet her. I was early, so I went inside to browse. I wasn't there too long before the door opened and in walked the girl with the beautiful face I recognized from our growing up years. She had a big smile on. She was a strapping woman with her 5'10" frame and power in her walk with a presence that absolutely overtook you. Her hair was a little darker than I remembered. She wore tight fitting jeans and a see-through button-down shirt with a pink camisole underneath, and she smelled like she bathed in lavender. She wore glasses now that made her look studious. She really looked good.

152

"Jan, you look wonderful."

"Thank you, so do you, Kate. I've missed you so." We hugged tightly and for a long time. "How is your dad, Kate?"

"He's well. He remarried last year. We all love her. He's retired now and lives in Quincy, Massachusetts." We had our arms around each other's waist.

"How are your folks?" Kate asked.

"They're good."

"And your brothers and sisters?"

"Everyone is doing well and they send their love." She tightened her hold on me and leaned her head on my shoulder.

"Come let me show you the view from the top floor." She grabbed my hand and pulled me with her. "I have so much to tell you," and she squeezed my hand. "Where is your suitcase?"

"I just have my shoulder bag and backpack."

"You travel light, girlfriend." We smiled at each other. "Charlie called me when you left to say you were on the train. He sounds happy."

"He is. He's been dating a German girl and they plan to marry when he gets out of the military." "I'm so happy for him." Kate was good friends with him, too, but I do think he was beguiled by her.

We took the stairs to the top floor and went to the window. Kate still had my hand but took it in both of her hands.

"I have something to tell you, love," as she kissed my hand.

"What's that?"

"I've met someone."

Immediately the words relationship, lover, commitment flashed through my thoughts. I found myself talking in my head, be positive, she's happy, and we both love each other no matter what! "Oh, Kate, I'm so happy for you. Tell me about your someone." She gave me a quick hug and kiss.

"We've been together for almost a year. I met her through a friend at Ghent."

I felt like I'd been hit by a truck. Suddenly, I flashed on the memory of Kate going off to Brown University. It was a big deal and I was so proud of her. Then without warning my brain, took a U-turn and I found myself thinking about that summer after sixth grade. I tried to follow her story. We left the book store and went to get a bite to eat. The rest of the afternoon and evening, I was resigned to be supportive and loving, but I so very much longed for her passionate kisses and to feel her body next to mine. We laughed and had a good time, but my heart felt a kind of sadness.

Kate took a little time off from school but eventually finished her Ph.D. One evening in early April, Justine called to tell me that Kate and her partner Elspeth were killed on March 30th, 1990 when their car went off a mountain road in Austria. I could not comprehend it. I cried for days. Justine also told me that Kate had written a letter to me when they lived in Rome. For some reason, it was never mailed but just tucked away. She told me it was written in 1968.

"Would you like me to read it or send it."

"I think send it."

After several days, I went through a box of old photos and letters and found a picture of Kate and I holding very tightly to each other, flanked by Justine and Dawn, with Kerry and Carla and Sue and Maggie surrounding Kate in back. It was taken the evening of our fateful sleep out. The tent stood in the back ground with Kate holding a brown grocery bag, and the writing on the back was "Mr. Cavanaugh's Playboys!" I put the picture up on the dresser mirror, stood back, and looked at it again, smiled and cried at the memory.

Chapter Fourteen

My Life in Plaid

I held the letter in my hand. Justine found it in Kate's belongings and sent it to me. It was written in 1968. I ran my fingers over the address: Janet Jacobs 705 Lee St., Rome, NY 13440. Then over the return address, where Kate's name was, as though by touching the print, I could bring her back. Kate Hart 707 Lee St., Rome, NY 13440. I pressed the envelope to my nose and lips and remembered that very difficult time. I had just discovered that I loved Kate beyond any love I knew up until then, yet I was angry at her for her hurtful and reckless behavior. The feelings came flooding back as though I was right there and then in the thick of it again.

The love that I felt for her and the memories were the only things I could hold on to. Growing up together and finally discovering our love, loving her, hadn't changed. I opened the letter. Ripping the envelope felt somewhat like destroying part of the memory. I pulled the letter out and started reading her 14-year old script:

Dear Jan,

I hope you can forgive me. I acted very badly and I know I've hurt your feelings. I just wanted to feel what it would be like to kiss a boy. I know I like kissing you better than Joe, and anyway, I love you. Why don't you come over

Friday night. My dad works late, so we can have some fun.

Please remember that I will always care about you. You are my best friend and I love you. You will always be in my heart, and when I'm away from you, my heart will miss you.

With love,

Kate

I thought for a second "have some fun" was our code phrase for sex. I started to smile a little and remembered that she always signed her letters, "my heart misses you – Kate." My eyes filled with tears. I looked at the writing for the longest time. In my mind's eye, I could see her writing the letter, and I imagined she was probably crying. We all know when we've done something wrong, gone a little too far, and hurt someone we care about. She knew. I folded the letter carefully and put it back in the envelope.

On March 30th, 1990, Kate and her partner Elspeth were killed when the car they were driving was pushed off the road and over a cliff by an avalanche. Her sister Justine called to tell me the details of her death. It was horrific. Kate's car was eventually found several days later, crushed, as were their bodies. I imagined the terror they must have felt as they were swept over the cliff, dragged by the avalanche. Justine and their father flew to Austria to identify her body and arrange to bring Kate to Massachusetts, where she would be buried. Justine called when she and her father returned. She told me quietly on the phone one night from her father's house that her father broke down and cried when he identified the body. She had never seen him cry.

"Kate's body will be flown to Quincy, Massachsetts," Justine told me, "Will you be able to come back for the service on the 12th of April?" I said I would.

We got off the phone and I tried to remember what Robert Hart looked like on Lee Street. He was so incredibly handsome. He looked just like Cary Grant. I had a hard time thinking of him as an older man in his 70's with gray hair and lines on his face. I called the airline right away. When my flight was booked, I opened a photo album and pulled some more pictures of Kate out and a lock of her beautiful hair that I saved. Crying was what I did most days and nights. I felt lost in my world, at the moment, where Kate would never call again and we would never exchange "I love you's."

Mindy and Tanya were the youngest Hart sisters. Mindy wore glasses almost from the moment she was born. She had soft brown hair and beautiful eyes like Kate. She was easy to laugh and talk like Kate but was much quieter and less dramatic than her. Tanya looked just like her older sister, Justine, and had a face full of freckles and very blond hair. She was as quiet as Mindy.

I called Mindy, who still occasionally communicated with my sister Joan. I spoke to an adult but couldn't picture the face of an adult. I pictured that very little smiling girl with the glasses. Kate and Mindy were unusually close, and it was clear that Mindy was feeling the loss of her sister much more than her other siblings.

"Oh, Jan, I can't believe this has happened. I don't know anyone who was ever killed by an avalanche! This is just so bizarre." Her voice cracked a bit.

"Are you going to Quincy? Justine says my father is having difficulty managing."

"Yes, I'm going. How are you doing, Mindy?" She stopped and sucked air and spoke with sobs. "I just can't believe it."

"I know," I said softly more to myself. We spoke for about 20 more minutes and then hung up, expecting to see each other at the service. Tanya was on her way back to Quincy from Flagstaff. Dawn was the only one I hadn't talked to yet. Justine had informed me some time ago Dawn had converted to Mormon.

"What does that mean," I had asked her.

"Well she doesn't spend holidays with us anymore. She doesn't celebrate them. She doesn't have a TV, or anything along those lines, and doesn't speak on the phone to chat, just to conduct business."

I gave up the idea of calling her. I had a hefty day at work tomorrow, so I pulled on my pajamas and fixed myself some cream of wheat and milk and went to bed. When I flipped off the lights, I tossed and turned and finally started to piece together a memory from our summers.

We ran wild, got up in the morning, and didn't come back home until dark when my father stood at the end of the driveway and whistled for us. One afternoon we spent in their house while their dad was at work. They told me stories about their mother and father. I was particularly interested in them since I'd only seen their mother twice in the year and a half that they lived in Rome. She was a really angry woman and the girls referred to her very softly as "sick" when describing her. One time she caught Kate and I kissing in her bedroom.

"What are you doing, Kate?" she screamed at us. "Get out here and stop that!"

I thought we were going to be in trouble, but she just yelled at us, told me to go home, and that was that. Days later she went back to the hospital that she was in. That was the first time I saw her.

The second time she was screaming at Mindy. We were sitting on the front step and we heard Mindy start to cry. Justine stepped in and tried to calm their mother down, Kate got up, went in, put her arm around Mindy's shoulders, and gently steered her outside to sit on the front step with us. We all stayed out of doors until Mr. Hart got home, and the next day, she was gone for good. I looked at the clock. It said 2:06 AM, I fell asleep.

On April 9th, I arrived in Quincy at four in the afternoon. Justine and Mindy picked me up at the airport. Justine introduced me to Mindy as an adult. The last time I saw her, she was five years old. Even without identification, I would have recognized her as one of the Hart sisters, but it was a little uncanny how much she resembled Kate. At one point, Mindy caught me staring at her.

She smiled and said, "I look a lot like Kate, don't I."

"Yes, you do," I said.

"I know; everyone tells me that." We drove to their father's house. Her father and his wife Julie greeted me. We hugged and exchanged greetings.

I looked at her father and said, "Mr. Hart, I'm so very sorry."

He acknowledged my condolence with a nod. He took my hand, just as Kate used to do, and for a moment, I felt Kate. He very carefully put his other hand over the top of mine and held my hand in a warm embrace. It was so reminiscent of her that I began to cry.

Over the next couple of days, people, mostly their family and our friend Charlie, came to Quincy for the service. I was more than a little glad to see Charlie. He was a comfort to me. He was a good and long-time friend that knew Kate and me very well. Justine had asked me to speak, along with Charlie and several others, including all her sisters. Mindy's speech was probably the most moving to me. She spoke of Kate's strength and her humor. I had written mine out, starting with a school picture Justine gave me of their first year of school in Montauk, Long Island. She sent one of all the girls, Kate, Dawn, herself, Mindy, and Tanya. There was Kate in her school dress, smiling, looking very confident with her beautiful head of auburn hair and dreaming of what university she would attend. She was in 9th grade. I talked about how outgoing and kind she was. It was all true; she spoke to girls in the neighborhood and often included them in our games. It didn't matter how rich or poor they were, popular or not, cute or homely, fat or skinny they were; all the girls mattered to her and she made sure that the boys behaved themselves around all of us. She was a budding feminist and we all knew it. When I looked out at the crowd, I saw Justine smiling and crying. Then I spoke about our friendship and what a genuine, delightful, and kind friend she was, how our friendship had weathered all these years, and how it was something I treasured. I put that at the end of my speech, and it was a good decision because I began to cry as I spoke.

I rode back to Mr. Hart's house with Justine, wishing that I could see her just one more time. To push her hair back, feel her kisses, and lie next to her. The next day was kind of a blur. We went to the cemetery and her casket was lowered into the ground. People picked up a handfuls of dirt and dropped it in the grave. I brought a sweater that Kate left behind when they moved the fall of 9th grade. It was navy blue and had her name embroidered inside. "Kate Hart." I had no reason to keep it all these years, but I did. I'd asked Justine if I could perhaps drop that in the grave and she said it would be alright. I walked up to the grave, kissed the sweater, and dropped it in.

I went home to San Francisco very soon after the ceremony, exhausted and feeling like I had the life energy sucked out of me. I had cried so much lately, I thought I probably couldn't conger up any tears, even if my life depended upon it. I stayed home from work for the next couple of days. The following day, I just laid in bed with the radio on and did nothing all day but think of her. In the evening, I received a call from Charlie.

"Hey, sugar."

"Hi."

"You feeling as miserable as I am?"

"Yes, I am."

"I think she would have liked your speech, Jan."

"Yeah, I guess."

"Listen, I'm scheduled to go back to Tacoma in the morning, but I thought I would spend a couple of days in San Francisco with you. I've talked to Terry and she's ok with it. Her sister is helping her with the kids."

"You know, I would really like that, Charlie. Is it going to cost you a ton to change your flight because I can help you with the cost."

"No, it's all good. I'm coming in at 12:32 PM tomorrow."

"What flight number?"

"2554."

"I'll pick you up, see you then."

For the first time in a couple of days, I felt calm. I fell asleep until about 9 AM the next morning. I got up, got dressed, had some breakfast, and left at 11:00 to pick up Charlie. I met Charlie when I worked at Griffiss Air Force Base in Rome, and we became good friends. During one of Kate's visits to Rome, I introduced him to her. He was quite taken with her, as most people were. She gently informed him that she was interested in woman, but she would like to be his friend. He was disappointed but good natured about being rebuffed.

"I should have figured out that you two were together when you told me that you liked girls."

Charlie ended up falling for a German gal while he was stationed in Germany. Her name was Krisi. They were madly in love, but Krisi contracted an aggressive form of breast cancer. She only lived two years. While visiting me in Rome, New York, several years after Krisi's death, I introduced Charlie to Terry and they dated, fell in love, married, and had three little girls, Anne, after Terry's mother, Kyle, and Martine.

Terry was one of nine kids. We became friends when my parents bought the house on Lee Street. across from her house. I was five and Terry was four. She was a little shorter than me, and with her mother being Irish and her father Italian, she had this great combination of the two. Her hair was very red and light brown, almost a strawberry blonde, but her skin was a deep brown in the summer. As we grew up, I thought Terry was very sexy. Kate had included her a couple of times in one of our tent sleepovers, but Terry and I had been having tent sleepovers with our friends Kerry and Sue long before Kate arrived in the neighborhood.

I went around the circle a couple of times at SFO before I spotted him. He looked relaxed and calm and smiled his beautiful smile as I drove to the curb. He was such a handsome guy. I jumped out and ran to hug him.

160

"I'm so glad you're here." The parking cops came walking down the sidewalk screaming at us, so we loaded his bag and took off.

"Where do you want to go?" he asked. I thought for a minute.

"How about down to the marina."

I could use some big distractions and there were plenty there. I was so grateful for his company. As we spoke to each other, the tempo of the conversation changed back and forth from humor to a depression that felt absolutely debilitating.

"Why'd you decide to detour to see me?"

"I saw you looking really down when you left for home, and to tell you the truth, I felt the same way. I just wanted to be with someone who knew her and could talk with me about her."

"Yeah, me, too."

"I figured," said Charlie.

The marina traffic was as crowed and difficult as always. We found a place on the street in front of Delancy's Restaurant. The day was warm for a spring day, even with a little breeze coming off the bay, but as is the case in most every day this time of year, you always needed a jacket by 3:00 PM.

Charlie sat, unusually quiet. I hesitated for a moment before getting out of the car and turned to him.

"What I wouldn't give for one more day with her. To lay in her arms, feel her breath on me, listen to her heart beat, touch her, smell her, kiss her."

I started to cry, and Charlie reached over and held me in his arms. He said nothing, just held me for a really long time. When he let go, he grabbed tissues and handed one to me and kept one. As I wiped my eyes, he did the same.

"Do you feel up to walking or would you rather go home?" he asked. What I felt like doing was getting drunk.

"Let's go to the Castro and get some dinner and get drunk at Harvey's."

"You're on, babe." We took off and I hit 60 mph, driving some stretches of Dolores Street.

"If you slow this fucking car down, sweetheart, I'll buy the first two rounds." I started to break for the light and drifted to a stop right next to a cop.

"He's a gay boy, Charlie. Tell him you like his tats."

The light changed, and we took off going in tandem with the cop.

Charlie relaxed a bit and I said, "I wanted you to make friends in case he was inclined to give us a ticket."

"You make friends, wild woman."

"He doesn't want to do me, Charlie, he likes boys. Didn't you see the way he smiled at you? You have a responsibility, Mr. Harris, to paste on that come fuck me look on to keep us ticket free, so I can drive in the manner to which I've become accustomed!"

Charlie laughed, "You're so twisted."

We turned down 18th and then onto Castro. It was a zoo, traffic and people everywhere. I ducked into the parking lot behind the Castro Theater and we waited only about ten minutes for a space. We locked up and walked to Harvey's. It was our lucky trip because we scored a table right at a window as we walked in.

"This place is interesting," Charlie said, practically yelling.

"Yeah, just don't have to use the restroom, it's smaller than an airplane and twice as dirty."

We had a meal, listened to the music, and did a few hours of people watching without really talking. It was the best kind of distraction. I got very drunk and felt sad in a tolerable way. When it came time to leave, Charlie took the keys and drove us home to Concord.

We pulled into the driveway.

"You painted your house."

"I had to, it was starting to look really bad."

"Did you hire lesbians to do the job?"

"No, I hired a couple of gay boys."

"Is that why it's so perfect?"

"That's right, it takes a lesbian to fix the place and a gay boy to make it pretty."

He laughed again. I opened the door, turned on the kitchen light, and put my purse on the table. "Charlieeee, would you like a beer?"

"If I'm going to keep up with you, I'll have several." I snorted out a laugh. Charlie went to the living room, put on some music, and lit a fire while I got a couple of beers and some chips. "Charlie, you know that Kate was with Elspeth for eight years?"

"Yes, I knew that. You felt every one of them, didn't you?" he said as he sat next to me and stroked my shoulder.

"Yes. I can't believe she's gone."

"I know, love."

"We can never know our fate."

"You two gals had a complicated relationship. How many years did you know each other?"

"We met in 1968, 22 years."

"You were like an old married couple, even when you were 15 and Kate was 17."

"I suppose."

"Are you still going out with, what's her name, Theresa?"

"We never really went out. I met her at the bar in Walnut Creek. She's really just someone to have sex with, that's all."

"Is that what you really want?"

"I'm ok with that."

"Really, really!? I know you pretty well, and I'd say you're lying, love." I didn't respond. "Is it that she's not Kate?"

"Nobody is Kate, Charlie, except Kate."

"That's it, isn't it? You can't find another Kate?"

"Charlie, please, why are you trying to pick a fight? You're being mean."

"I'm not, but I'm worried about you."

"Why?"

"Because you've had all these short-term noncommittal relationships ever since Kate and Elspeth got together."

I thought about it and ticked off relationships in my head. He was right. I said nothing.

"I've gotta pee, I'll be back." When I returned, he was pulling a beer out of the fridge.

Charlie was like a dog with a bone.

He turned to me and said, "So, why do you waste your time with women you're not really interested in?"

"Charlie, come the fuck on, you're ruining a good drunk."

"Just talk with me about this, Jan. I'm really worried about you." I got up and grabbed another beer from the fridge, went to the living room, and sat on the floor in front of the fire.

"Alright, have at it, let's get this done and over with. You first, Charles."

I could tell he was concerned, but I felt that if I reassured him that he would leave things alone. Boy, was I ever wrong.

"Did you ever talk to Kate like this?"

"I did. We had a long talk."

"What did she say?"

"She told me that she loved you very much."

I sat upright and said, "But I wasn't there at the right time or at all?"

"It's just the way it worked out. You both had very different lives, Jan. You loved Kate. I get that she was the love of your life. And despite losing her several times, when she left for school and met other woman, when she and Elspeth became partners, Kate loved you."

This was getting to me and I began to tear up.

"Just think about this for a moment. For all that you and Kate had, and it was a lot, and for all that you meant to each other, it was to the exclusion of anyone who might have meant something to you. You were kind and altruistic to Elspeth, but you lived and loved only for Kate. The thing is, Jan, I get it. When I lost Krisi, I didn't want to venture out anywhere with anyone for a long time. I felt that I would never find that kind of love ever again, and even if I did, that I would be untrue to Krisi's memory if I pursued a relationship."

I never expected to hear this at all, much less from Charlie.

"Is that what you think I'm doing? Avoiding relationships that mean anything?"

"Yeah, you know you are."

"God, Charlie, I really miss her." I thought about a phrase that my father would say to us, "Nowhere are there more hiding places than in one's heart."

I was tired and sad, drunk, and Charlie's hammering at the protective barrier around my heart made me feel all those things even more keenly, and I was lonely as well. I hoped it all would be gone by morning.

Charlie held out his hand, "Come on, sleep will help."

"How 'bout you?"

"I might sleep in front of the fire."

"Ok."

I took off my jeans and slid into bed. He pulled the covers over me, kissed me on the forehead, and turned out the light. In the dark, I could hear the fire crackling. I raised my hand, putting the palm of my hand against my lips and whispered, "My heart misses you, Kate Hart."

I was tired when I woke. I pulled on my robe and walked into the kitchen to find Charlie sitting at the table with coffee and the Bay Times I had just picked up.

He looked up, "Good morning, love."

"Good morning, Charlie."

"How are you feeling, love?"

"I feel like shit."

"I'm not surprised."

I padded down the hall, and when I returned, Charlie was sipping his coffee.

"Found an ad for you in the Bay Times Love."

"Come on, It's too early for that." I made myself a cup of coffee and brought that and the phone to the table.

"Making a date?"

"No, cancelling one. I was supposed to see Theresa tonight."

"Oh."

"Aside from only purchasing dental dams for her, she isn't even all that interesting."

"Hmm."

"It all seems so surreal. The sun is up and people are starting their day and my best friend in the whole world isn't even on the earth anymore."

"I know what you mean," said Charlie.

"Did you ever visit her in Belgium, Charlie?"

"Krisi and I did only once before we left for the states. They were living in Ghent and looking for a place outside the city. She had just finished school."

He took a couple of big gulps of coffee.

"Did you ever spend time with Kate and Elspeth, Jan?"

"I met with them when they first got together and when they saw us off to Alaska. I…"

"You what?" he asked. I looked at him and wondered if he'd question my sanity.

"I wondered what they were like together in bed."

"Hmm."

"Sick, huh?"

"Seems natural for a former lover who is still very much in love to go there." We both smiled. "You know," Charlie said. "she thought about you a lot."

"You think?"

"I think. We'd sit around in the evening with Kate and Elspeth and Kate would tell stories of you when you played baseball or football with the boys and how you both could out run them or beat them up!"

"Oh god!" We both started to laugh.

"That was the first time," said Charlie, "that I heard about what a mafioso you both were. She also told me that she hurt your feelings one time and you decided to forgive her and so walked into the middle of a football game, grabbed her, and kissed her in front of everyone! You lesbians are a shameless lot." We laughed again. "She also told me she hoped you would make another trip over." I felt the stab of deep sadness again.

"Charlie, let's go into the city…"

"And do what?"

"Go climbing around Sutro Baths and have some lunch at Joe's Diner."

"Ok, race you to the car."

"That's not fair, you're dressed already!"

"You're such a baby."

I reached out to punch him and he grabbed my arm, spun me around, and smacked me on the butt.

"Get dressed."

"Be careful, I might like that!" I smiled at him and he raised his eyebrows.

We hiked at Sutro until we were good and cold. The fog hung on until almost one o'clock. We ate breakfast at Joe's. It was good and hearty and way cheaper than the cliff house next door. We talked more about Kate and Charlie's wife, Terry.

"Do you know we were together nearly two years before she told me anything about your summertime tent sleep-overs." I raised my eyebrows.

"I'm not surprised."

"You're not?"

"No, Charlie, it was the best kept secret on the block."

"What are you saying? They referred to you girls as a bunch of 'lezzies.'"

"Well, they did, but they didn't really know what was going on. The only ones who did were my brother Joe, and his friend, Matt Wells."

"Hmm," was the only thing Charlie said.

We changed gears and I asked Charlie about the kids.

"How old is Annie now?"

"She'll turn eight in a couple of months and Kyle will be six next month, and Martine is just recently four."

Terry found out she was pregnant when Charlie and I were on the road in Alaska, but she lost the baby. Shortly after, they learned that they were unable to have any more children.

We looked out the window at the ocean, turbulent and beautiful, the sun making the green color almost neon. Charlie was due to take off at 9:45 AM the following morning. I didn't want him to leave, but I would never tell him that. He was going back to the arms of his wife and children. I was going back to my house in Concord. Suddenly the lonely part was amped up. I longed for a lover and partner.

"What thoughts dragged you around the world?" Charlie said. I looked at him. "Where did you go, Jan?"

"Nowhere worth talking about. Charlie, how can I ever thank you for our time together?"

"You can come to Tacoma. Anne asks about you, but the others are too young to remember you. I haven't told you yet but perhaps you can visit us in Madrid as well?"

"As in Madrid, Spain?"

"That's it."

"Wow, how exciting."

"It is exciting, will you come to see us before we leave?"

"When are you leaving?"

"In June of next year."

We decided to head back to Concord. He packed his suitcase and came to my bedroom where I was making up my bed.

"I brought you something," and he handed me an envelope. I sat on the bed and opened it. He sat next to me. I reached in and pulled out a picture of Kate and me. We were holding tightly to each other and laughing hard. We were in our summer uniforms: short sleeve shirts, plaid shorts, and flip flops. On the back was written, "Kate and Jan, 1969." I looked at it and began to cry.

"Oh, Charlie, where did you find this?"

"Terry gave it to me, she thought you might like it."

"I love it. I'll call her to thank her." I turned it back over and said, "I remember this. We had two weeks of 'fun.'"

"Hmm," was all he said but gave me a sly smile. I hugged him.

"Thank you."

"You're welcome, love."

I saw Charlie, Terry, and the girls the following year in Tacoma. Anne was nine, Kyle, seven, and Martine, five.

"Your household must be interesting with three little girls."

"They keep us busy."

"You two are wonderful parents."

"Thank you," said Terry. Those little girls were smart, polite, and very precocious. Terry had encouraged them to make goodbye cards for me and they all handed me their card they made. I looked at them one at a time.

Anne wanted to know, "Will you visit us again?"

"I'll try." I opened her card last and inside she had written, "My heart will miss you."

"Oh, girls, the cards are beautiful."

I looked at Terry, who was smiling. I began to tear up. Charlie, stood there, grinning from ear to ear. I grabbed his arm and pulled him into a hug.

I could hear Kyle say, "Mommy, why is Jan crying?"

Terry responded with, "Because she is happy."

In June of that year Charlie and family left the states and settled in Madrid, his life-long dream. We talked on the phone a couple of times, but I never did make it to Madrid. I'd taken a new job in 1990 and I was hard pressed to take time off, and when I did two years later, I talked with Charlie on the phone early in the year and could tell from his speech that something was wrong. Every time I questioned him about it, he would down play it. I didn't press him. I figured he would tell me in his own time. I heard from Terry in late January of 1993 that Charlie had ALS and died in early January. I was shocked, but I remembered that he had terrible muscle spasms and was constantly having strength and coordination issues since the late 80's. I was inconsolable. He was a close connection to Kate and I loved him more than my own brothers. I felt guilty for not taking the time to visit him in Madrid.

Terry said, "He missed you, Jan. He hoped you would visit us here in Madrid. He loved you very much." Tears filled my eyes and I began to sob.

"I'm so sorry, Terry."

"Thank you, I'm sorry you lost your good friend. He was such a good man, Jan."

"I know."

"It was five years ago that you two took the trip to Alaska. The whole thing meant a lot to him. He was really touched that you wanted him to go with you."

"It was special to me that he agreed to. How long did he have ALS?"

"Shortly after we moved to Madrid, he began to display really drastic symptoms."

"Like what?"

"Loss of control of his muscles, particularly in his arms and hands. No one knew what we were dealing with for some time." I was shocked but clearly recalled that Charlie had trouble manipulating things with his hands when we were in Alaska.

"Terry, he had problems with the strength in his arms and hands when we were in Alaska."

"I'm not surprised."

"His voice," I said.

"Yes," said Terry "his voice and ability to speak at all was very much affected. They say that ALS ravages the body very quickly. We think that he had it about two years before we moved to Madrid."

I wanted to know how she was doing and how the girls were doing. They were having a difficult time, especially Anne, who was 11. Terry said that several of her brothers and both sisters were there supporting her at different times! Every one of her sibs had been over at least once, as well as her parents. We talked about an hour. When I got off the phone, I cried as much as I had on getting the news of Kate for days.

One evening, almost a year after Terry called to tell me about Charlie, I was running errands in the mall and they had Christmas music everywhere, when all of a sudden, a song by Cat Stevens came on, "Another Saturday night and I ain't got nobody…" I stopped in my tracks. I sat down and thought, that's so weird. That was Charlie's favorite song. He would sing it and become very animated. I sat down on a bench and felt an Arctic chill go through me. I can tell you for sure that Charlie was with me on that bench. I felt him so intensely that I could almost see him. As for the music, well, Charlie loved music and it was not outside the realm of possibilities that he would communicate with his favorite song. I sat on that bench talking, in my head, to my very dear friend. I didn't want the moment to end. I felt very comforted by that singular communication with Charlie.

Also in 1993, I got a call from Justine. Her father had passed just recently and the girl's biological mother the year before. Mindy was an RN living and working in Quincy and caring for Julie Hart, his second wife. I think at that point I just shut down. I couldn't bear to hear of one more death.

In 1994, I was working in San Francisco and living in Concord, a three hour commute each day. I had a 2,200 sq. ft. home with a big yard that required a lot of work. I was training two new employees, going to school, and volunteering for the Big Brother, Big Sister program. The only social aspect of my life was staying in the city on Thursday or Friday nights to have dinner and maybe a show with my friends or having them out for the weekend to visit. I really was lonely and wanted a relationship. So, my friend Glen suggested over and over that I place an ad in the gay newspaper, the Bay Times. It was the thing to do and I had been reading ads for a couple of months now. Finally, I wrote my own and the girl of my dreams answered it.

Her name was Jill and her voice was sexy and sweet. She met me for dinner near my work with a rose, and we hit it off immediately, making plans for the next date at my house, which was New Year's Day. We had a lot of "fun," and after several visits, decided to be exclusive to each other. I had moments when I thought of Kate, but it was different now. My new girlfriend made the butterflies in my stomach come to life. She was kind and easy to laugh and talk. We had a lot in common. I couldn't wait to see her again and frequently drove like a mad woman to get to where she was. One evening while watching the sun set at the Marina, I realized that I was head over heels in love with her. I told myself that over and over until I could tell it to her. I realized also that I wanted to spend the rest of my life with this exceptional and loving woman. So, on January 1st, 1997, we had a "commitment ceremony."

We booked the Swedenborgian Church in San Francisco and the Rec. Hall behind, hired a dress maker, caterer, cake maker, a woman to officiate at the ceremony, a photographer, and pianist to play for the ceremony and party afterward. I asked my good friend to sing at the ceremony, we purchased rings and wrote our vows, invited our family and friends, and had the time of our lives, agreeing that it was the best party we'd ever been to. We stayed at a hotel on the peninsula and flew off to Hawaii for a honeymoon.

When I woke that morning of the ceremony, I sat on the side of the bed and looked out over the Bay. It rained all night and was still raining but no matter; we were publicly declaring our love for each other this day, January 1st, 1997.

I silently thanked Kate for teaching me the depth that a person could love and Charlie for pulling me out of the hiding place in my heart. The last person to thank was the love of my life, Jill, for making it so easy for me to love her and feel I was loved in return.

The End, for now